THE CASE AGAINST ABORTION

A Logical Argument for Life

Lori Van Winden

LIGUORI
PUBLICATIONS

One Liguori Drive
Liguori, Missouri 63057-9999
(314) 464-2500

Imprimi Potest:
Stephen T. Palmer, C.SS.R.
Provincial, St. Louis Province
Redemptorist Fathers

Imprimatur:
Monsignor Maurice F. Byrne
Assistant Chancellor, Archdiocese of St. Louis

ISBN 0-89243-295-0
Library of Congress Catalog Card Number: 88-82302

Table of Contents

Dedication

This book is lovingly dedicated to my children, Kristi and Michael. In their tender way of savoring life's every offering I find daily inspiration. And I thank you, Ardy, for your unflagging confidence and support.

Foreword

On January 22, 1973, the Supreme Court of the United States discovered a new right in the Constitution — the right of a woman to end her pregnancy at any time in its course. Though the Court was vague as to where the Constitution had located this "fundamental right," it was nonetheless sure of its power to proclaim a constitutional mandate. Several scholars were quick to point out the illegitimacy of this claim; they labeled the establishment of this right as nothing less than "an act of raw judicial power."

The effects of this one judicial act have been devastating. Today almost every third baby conceived in America is killed by abortion, a total of over one and one-half million babies a year. Something has to be done to stop what the Second Vatican Council called an "abominable crime." Pope John Paul II, in his address to representatives of the Catholic Health Association in Phoenix, Arizona (September 14, 1987), reiterated traditional teaching, stating: "The church cannot fail to emphasize the need to safeguard the life and integrity of the human embryo and fetus. The human person is a unique composite — a unity of spirit and matter, soul and body, fashioned in the image of God and destined to live forever. Every human life is sacred because every human person is sacred. It is in the light of this fundamental truth that we see the great evil of abortion."

It was because she had taken this same basic truth to heart that Lori Van Winden, a young California wife and mother, decided to present THE CASE AGAINST ABORTION: A LOGICAL ARGUMENT FOR LIFE. She felt the need to unmask this "right," so mistaken in its foundations, so far-reaching in its evil consequences, and so deadly in its exercise.

After detailing the intricacies of prenatal development, after describing the methods of abortion, and after exposing the hollowness of the pro-abortion arguments, the author asks us to look at what she calls "The Abortion Mentality." It is her hope that this chapter will alert us to a present danger. She writes: "The [abortion] mentality looms like a dark cloud over us all. With each day of death that passes we are learning to live in its shadow. In fact, abortion has become so fused into our societal landscape that its pollutant effects are inescapable. They are everywhere — sometimes where we least expect to see them. In a nation where abortion is commonplace, these insidious influences seep into the crevices of daily existence, touching everyone in one way or another.

"All are in the grips of the mentality, not only the advocates of abortion but idle pro-lifers as well who feel helpless to change it. With the draw of a vortex, the mentality sucks into its powerful current anything and anyone around it — forever changing not only a way of life but a way of looking at life."

It isn't easy to escape from this noxious atmosphere. The message of this book is that, though the situation is desperate, it is not hopeless: "God help us, there's a better solution out there — and it lies not in despair but in hope, not in conflict but in concern, not in death but in life." I pray that this book will fulfill the highest hopes of the author — that its readers will come to realize that "there is no higher or more noble cause which deserves our dedication."

+ John L. May
Archbishop of St. Louis
President of the National
Conference of Catholic Bishops

Preface

Human beings, as they move about their world, constantly confront risk:

Freeway motorists live with the menace of drunk drivers.

Airline passengers, every time they buckle up, face the possibility of a catastrophic accident.

Any malfunction at a nuclear power plant has the potential of exposing those living or working nearby to dangerous levels of radiation.

Travelers in Europe and the Middle East have to be wary of the threat of terrorism.

Miners, high-rise construction workers, chemists handling hazardous materials, and many others, including professional athletes, regularly chance injury in their occupations.

It is now known that the most perilous locale on earth is not any of the above. It is not on the highway or in a plane at 30,000 feet. It is not in the vicinity of a nuclear power plant, or on a ship in the Mediterranean or the Persian Gulf. Nor is it in the depths of a coal mine, atop the frame of a towering skyscraper, or on the athletic field.

No, statistically the most dangerous place in the world is the human womb. What nature had designed as its most protected citadel has become an extremely active death chamber, a place where 1.5 million children die annually.[1]

A fact of this gravity is not without certain repercussions on the human condition. Abortion is undoubtedly the most explosive and divisive issue of our day.[2] Along its ascent to the level of epidemic it has been the subject of many heated debates and a profusion of books, pamphlets, and other publications.

Traditionally, an abortion has been defined as the premature ejection of the fetus from the mother's body. Although this formal definition encompasses both spontaneous abortion, or miscarriage, and induced abortion, this writing concerns itself only with the meaning and implications of the latter occurrence.

Hereafter, any usage of or reference to the term abortion is understood to mean the deliberate extraction of the fetus from the womb.

There is a temptation to consider the merits of abortion on its usefulness to the perceptible world. What is really needed, though, in pursuit of the truth, is an appraisal of broader scope — one that attempts to take in the whole sweep, including abortion's more recondite influences. Indeed, there is more to this practice than "meets the eye." It was in this spirit that *The Case Against Abortion: A Logical Argument for Life* was written.

Let it be known up front that I am pro-life in that I believe human life to be unconditionally sacred. If this allegiance of mine was in force at the inception of this work, its presence was positively overwhelming by the point of completion. The more I learned of abortion, the more I pondered its meaning, the more devoted to the pro-life cause I became.

This book begins with a look at conception and prenatal development, the understanding and appreciation of which are a cornerstone in the pro-life way of thought.

The methods of abortion are discussed in some detail, followed by a dismantling review of the most frequently used pro-abortion arguments.

Then, inasmuch as they are integrally associated with the procedure, the physical and emotional effects of abortion on the mother receive brief treatment.

To explore the troubled area of abortion's social ramifications, the chapter dealing with the abortion mentality is offered. This chapter, particularly, might impel the reader to serious thought, as it did this writer, while it bares the parochial mentality which holds us all hostage.

The final chapter covers the conditions which were, in this author's eyes, the progenitors of legalization and also suggests the urgency of a morally recuperative path — one that will hew, universally, to the respect-for-life imperative.

Abortion is not solely a religious matter and, although Bible quotes and references are used intermittently throughout the book, the reader will soon discover that being pro-life is a sociocultural issue, of as much concern to the humanist as it is to the religiously inclined.

Thus, the main thrust of this writing is directed not only at my cohorts in faith but also at all who share in this common bond of humanity in the hopes that they will see, as I have seen, that there is no higher or more noble cause which deserves our dedication.

CHAPTER ONE

A New Life

The human fascination with conception dates back to the earliest days. The idea of reproducing oneself from elements invisible to the naked eye was a source of great awe and the basis for some quite imaginative theorizing. Many wondered, argued, and speculated about it. Ongoing attempts were initiated to procure it, prevent it, and control it. But only recently unraveled were the intense biological intricacies of the instant when human propagation reaches its zenith.

Over the years, particularly during the last thirty or so, advancements in medical science have begun to lift the veil, thereby revealing much of the mystery enshrouding humankind's inaugural moment. Even so, conception remains somewhat of an enigma.[1]

Conception

During her lifetime, the average woman will produce upwards of 400 mature ova, the tiny female genetic storehouses, at the rate of one per month, while her male counterpart will generate enormous quantities of his genetic packages, or sperm, continuously during his adult years.

Prior to conception, great armies of sperm are released into the woman's body. Swimming purposefully amid uterine tides and currents, their ranks diminish as they search for the ripe ovum (which is receptive to fertilization for a matter of hours, or one day at best, before perishing). Only the most vital sperm survive the five- or six-inch voyage to the Fallopian tube where fertilization can hope to take place. It is a journey that lasts several hours, culminating in the penetration of the egg by a single sperm.

When the ovum and sperm so conjoin, a new cell called the zygote is formed and conception has occurred. It is a moment of infinite implications and prodigious possibilities as the genetic material of the mother and father is interfused.

Each parent cell houses many thousands of genes apportioned along forty-six string-like chromosomes, which are the very threads of transferable biological information. The ovum and sperm contribute half of their respective genetic arrangements at fertilization. In an intimate chemical exchange, genes from the father and mother amalgamate to create the formula for a new and inimitable person. The very gist of human existence and the familial link with forefathers and future descendants is marvelously realized.

Gone are the separate male/female cells. What comes into being at that moment is a brand new, genetically unique human person, set apart by a code of heritage from the countless billions who ever have and ever will inhabit the earth.

His or her every physical characteristic: sex, hair and eye color, height, blood type, birth marks, nose shape, and feet size (and even certain emotional predisposals) have already been determined as bodily formation of the new being gets under way. Everything needed to facilitate the full and complete development of a mature human is present forthwith in the tiny zygote. No other bits or pieces need ever be added. The components for a heart to supervise circulation, for a brain to reason, think, and feel, and even for new reproductive cells (looking to the next generation!) are all included. As everything small or large, simple or complex must have a beginning, so a human person containing billions of cells originates from a single, self-propelling cell.

Independent of one another, the sperm and the ovum contain "life" — insofar as the rest of bodily cells contain life. Yet, if their purpose of procreation is not fulfilled, they die and are passed from the body. When the goal of fertilization is realized, what marvels ensue!

Together, the cells of reproduction have the power to initiate the dynamic process that is life. The melding of the two into a new third entity provides all the components and driving forces necessary to spur on the development of a baby, to hurl a new being down the one-way paths of physical and emotional growth. It is clear that the miracle lies not in either the sperm or ovum individually, but in the union of the two and the transformation that results. Given this, conception can be accurately dubbed the single most biologically significant moment in any one person's lifetime.

Despite this — despite the fact that conception may very well be the most remarkable feat evidenced by human beings — it is often viewed as little more than a mundane bodily function or, at worst, an untimely happenstance. A possible explanation for this may be the extraordinary number of times it occurs. In this country, a new human being is conceived several times each minute. But perhaps great frequency is not the only factor that promotes lack of appreciation for this phenomenon. For better or worse, technology looms large over the involuted workings of human reproduction. That modern science allows conception to occur through artificial means in the mother's body, and even in the impersonal atmosphere of a laboratory, may divert attention from the splendor of this prolific phenomenon.

As we turn our focus from the biological implications of conception to its spiritual significance, I can assure you that it is far from mundane and anything but a happenstance. Passage after passage of Scripture communicates the concept of a divine awareness and involvement surrounding the child before birth.

Before I formed you in the womb I knew you,
    before you were born I dedicated you (Jeremiah 1:5).

Your hands have formed me and fashioned me;
    . . . you fashioned me from clay!
Did you not pour me out as milk,
    and thicken me like cheese?
With skin and flesh you clothed me,
    with bones and sinews knit me together.
Grace and favor you granted me,
    and your providence has preserved my spirit.
                                        (Job 10:8-12).

From this understanding, acceptance of the unborn's importance as a person in the whole of God's master plan most easily flows. Every person has an integral role in the divine plan and possesses a supreme contextual worth — even before the actual unification of body and soul.

Perhaps no other passage so explicitly conveys this sentiment of God as imparter of the soul and master of divine destiny as Psalm 139:

Truly you have formed my inmost being;
    you knit me in my mother's womb. . . .
My soul also you knew full well;
    nor was my frame unknown to you
When I was made in secret,
    when I was fashioned in the depths of the earth.
Your eyes have seen my actions;
    in your book they are all written;
    my days were limited before one of them existed.
                                        (Psalm 139:13-16)

Clearly, then, God's love for each person exists long before the instant of conception. For, what lies between a conceptus and a seven-pound newborn? Between this same newborn and an octogenarian? The answer, of course, is time — that tireless continuum that connects one event to another, as the first day of kindergarten to graduation day, and a conception to an eightieth birthday. Yet, time is but a mere dimension of our world. It, like all else, is the creation of an ageless God — a God whose wisdom is infinite, whose power is almighty, and whose love is eternal, transcending the temporal limitations of human existence. He sees the same person at conception, at birth, and eighty years beyond. He is above the perimeters of time as we know it and the confining perspective of "now."

This leads us to the happy conclusion that each human person is not a product of blind chance walking aimlessly through a fortuitous existence. But, because he or she has a preordained role, because the Supreme Being has a purposeful plan for this individual, the essence of his or her conception takes on a meaning of vigorous import. It heralds the embodiment of an eternal soul.

For some, perhaps, this definition of conception may require a walk on a shaky stretch of faith. But for others, this other-worldly view shares a wonderfully complementary relationship with the verdicts of biological science — as the moment of full and complete physical and spiritual homogenization. No other single instant during prenatal or postnatal existence, not even birth, carries the dramatic impact of spontaneous "life."

Indeed, and despite scientific revelations, a sacral mystery still encircles the moment of conception when God "breathes" life into a new human form.

In his hand is the soul of every living thing,
    and the life breath of all mankind (Job 12:10).

All that one is and can ever hope to become has its origins at the introduction of sperm and egg. Conception is the very springboard to life.

Yet, it is just the beginning. As we shall see in the following section, conception sets the stage for a spectacular evolutionary process, the design and organization of which can be likened to creation itself.

Fetal Development

It is a competent mechanism, the human body — complex, wonderfully efficient, and programmed for self-preservation.

We evidence this in the way a young girl blossoms into a mature woman and a spindly young boy into a man; in the way a cut finger will immediately set about the task of healing itself; in the power of the immune system to attack intrusive cells and foreign materials and ward off disease; in the ability of the respiratory and circulatory systems to adjust to different levels of physical activity. The interdependent components and the delicately balanced functions of the human body could fill volumes. How does it all begin? How is such a detailed consortium of synergetic parts fashioned?

It is quite a remarkable orchestration of formation, growth, and perpetual maintenance that begins at conception and continues on until death. Undoubtedly, the sojourn in the womb — a microcosm of evolution — is the most industrious and fascinating interlude of all.

We are fortunate that today more is known about the first months of life than ever before. Partly through microscopic investigation and photography, modern medical technology has given firsthand witness to the once mystifying stint of human development that takes place in the womb. Exhaustive research by embryologists and scientists has paved the way to a keener and more complete understanding of the revolution that occurs inside the uterus of an expectant mother.[2]

However, despite these new insights, the exact hows and whys and the purposeful motivation behind this endogenous process still elude us and perhaps are beyond the scope of knowledge that scientific knowledge can deliberate.

Realizing that during prenatal maturation millions upon millions of events must happen in synchronized succession, what follows is a highlighted account of the developments and landmarks of growth on the road from the human zygote to a seven-pound, birth-ready infant.[3] (Author's note: In this section I decided, for simplicity's sake, to use masculine pronouns and adjectives. If so inclined, the reader may substitute feminine nouns and modifiers in reference to the developing baby.)

Week #1:

While his cells divide and multiply, the new being travels slowly through the Fallopian tube, eventually burrowing his way into the warm, spongy inner lining of the uterus to establish a source of protection and nourishment. This act of implantation, sometimes called "nesting," occurs on about the sixth day following conception. Here, in the fertile resort of the womb, he will continue to grow until he becomes too large for this environment and must move into another one through birth.

A veritable little workshop in only a dot-sized cluster of cells, he has begun to carefully follow the genetic code dispatched by his parents. Through a series of chemically emitted signals and responses, he is in the first stages of a singular regimen of complex development. The efforts of the first week of life transform the minute zygote into a being containing hundreds of cells with the number doubling about every twelve hours.

Week #2:

In a wonderful feat of self-protection, some of the baby's cells form a fluid-filled sac around him called the amnion. The placenta and umbilical cord, vital links to oxygen and nutrition, and agents to manage the transfer of waste materials from child to mother, are in rudimentary stages of formation.

Still deceptively small (he's no larger than a grain of rice), his size perhaps belies the ambitious resolve being fulfilled within. Already, cells which will eventually form each part and organ of his body are being sorted and classified. This process, known as "differentiation," is not fully understood. It is known, though, that at the controls of this prescripted plan of action are the genes of the parents which govern the cells' arrangement. In this way, groups of cells from the original cluster are "instructed" in specific duties: some will form the nervous system; another group, the liver and digestive system; still another combination will initiate development of the heart and other components of the circulatory system. The makings of each body part are being readied. As time goes on, these generalized groups of cells subdivide and become increasingly more intricate and specialized as they work toward completion of their assigned goals.

However, at this point, there is still much to be done.

Week #3:

As differentiation continues, the child's brain and spinal cord begin to take shape. Also evolving are the liver and kidneys and the preliminary tissue of the vertebrae called somite. The end of this week witnesses the first pulsations of the heart.

Week #4:

The child's heart beats quite regularly now, at a pace of 60 to 70 times per minute, and his facial structure is well under way. Although he is 10,000 times greater in size than when he first came into existence one month ago, he is still tinier than a kidney bean.

Week #5:

Dark "spots," soon to be eyes, are perceptible. Within a short time lids will seal themselves closed temporarily as the delicate development of the optical organs is in progress.

Perfect little hands are forming at the ends of the arm "buds" which sprouted only days ago. The child's lower extremities lag slightly behind in comparable development. In about a week or so, the knobby projections at the end of the torso will yield his feet. As an infant first learns control of his eyes, then his arms and hands, and finally his legs and feet as he begins to walk, so patterned is pre-birth development: from the head down.

Weeks #6-8:

During these weeks brain expansion is quite pronounced. As early as day forty brain waves can be detected and recorded. These electrical impulses direct existing and developing bodily functions. The baby has a mouth with lips, a tongue, and buds for 20 milk teeth. Each minute his heart propels blood through the growing network of vessels 130 times. Real bone cells are replacing the cartilage which formed earlier as a preparatory mold.

The baby moves gracefully in his buoyant world — floating peacefully one minute and performing flips the next. As the muscle sets and nervous system begin to work together, he becomes capable of response. If it were possible to touch the baby's nose at this point, he would flex his head backward. He is, in every sense, a structurally complete human baby. Growth and refinement are all that will take place throughout the remaining seven months or so before birth.

Month #3:

The child, now about four inches long, can turn his head, squint, swallow, breathe, curl his toes, kick, and wrinkle his forehead — quite noteworthy exploits for someone who could have lost himself in a thimble less than twelve weeks ago. Nails appear on his fingers and toes and he can boast his very own set of fingerprints. For a number of weeks the child's sense of feel has been growing more and more acute. A touch of his palm now would prompt him to tightly clench his fists. He has periods of wakefulness and sleep, and may even try to cry with his newly developed vocal cords, and actually would if his environment so allowed. I once read of an experiment performed on a pregnant woman wherein a bubble of air was injected into the sac of water surrounding her baby. At the times his face touched the pillow of air, the child actually did produce audible cries, often keeping his mother awake at night with the noise.

Month #4:

During this month the child grows to be about ten inches long. His heart pumps over six gallons of blood per day. With his newly operating ears, he is becoming accustomed to the swishing sounds of his watery environment and is comforted by his mother's voice. His sucking reflex is apparent as he often takes his thumb into his mouth.

Functioning completely now is the placenta. Nature's remarkable mediator, it allows the peaceful coexistence of beings with different blood types and separate genetic constitutions. It is thought that the reconciliatory powers of this organ might hold the secret to preventing rejection in transplant patients.

Months #5-6:

The baby's length continues to increase rapidly and he reaches about one and a half pounds in weight. He has favorite positions and may kick frantically if he can't get "comfortable."

Months #7-9:

The baby's heart now pumps 300 gallons of blood each day at a rate of 120-155 beats per minute. He comes to weigh over seven pounds and grows to be about 20 inches long. Blood pulses through the umbilical cord, which is about the same length as the child, at a speed of four miles per hour. Nature is preparing him for life in the outside world: Antibodies are stocked for protection against disease; an insulating layer of fat is produced underneath the skin in anticipation of the 20- to 30-degree drop in temperature he will experience at birth; his head is in a downward position, ready for the journey through the birth canal.

Nearly nine months have elapsed since conception. With pulsating energy, the unicellular zygote has been parlayed into an integrated body of several hundred million cells!

Of course, the child's process of development will not end at birth. He will continue to grow and mature until his late teen years. And even though after birth a child's length will better than triple by adulthood and his weight will increase by anywhere from 15 to 30 times, it seems a rather modest transformation when compared to that realized during the first nine months of his life.[4] If it were possible to allow an average man to grow at the dizzying pace of a child in utero, in nine months' time he would stand about four miles high and weigh in at a hefty 250 million tons!

When the long-awaited day finally arrives, it is believed the baby sends out "signals" to the mother's brain which, in turn, commences the labor process. The baby is expelled from her body by a series of strong uterine contractions. This marks the completion of the muffled existence in the womb and signifies the beginning of a brand new place to live — a diverse world of bright lights and colors, abrupt sounds, and distinctly contoured people and objects. There are places to see and things to explore, all to be experienced in due time. Just as the prenatal embryo gradually grew accustomed to his world and adjusted to his surroundings in the womb, so must he now adapt to the sharp contrasts and sensations of his post-birth environment.

CHAPTER TWO

Abortion
Techniques

A woman's physiology changes with the onset of pregnancy. Instinctively her body becomes a fortress to protect the new life within her. Her cervix, the muscular "support" of the womb, grows hard and closes to shield the developing child. Hormonal balances shift and her bodily functions work in consonance with the needs of the baby *in utero*.

The "optimal" abortion, therefore, must carefully bypass the roadblocks erected by the woman's natural defense system to achieve its intended result: fetal expulsion.

Methods of abortion vary.[1] Which is advisable in any given case is determined by such factors as the duration of the pregnancy, fetal size, and the mother's condition. What follows is a brief description of the most common procedures used to sunder the stringent physical bond between a mother and the infant in her womb.[2]

Suction Aspiration

This method begins with the vaginal insertion of a series of graduated instruments to stretch open the cervix, which is rigid and tightly closed during pregnancy. Next, a transparent plastic tube is introduced into the uterus. A knife-like edge on the tip of the tube slices and tears the baby to tiny pieces and is used to crush his head.

After the placenta is cut from the uterine wall a strong suction is applied. Twenty-five times more powerful than a vacuum cleaner, this suction forces the fragmentary remains through the hollow tube and into an awaiting container. Often, tiny legs, arms, feet, hands, and other identifiable parts of the baby are visible in the flowing morass of blood and tissue.

Suction aspiration is used in a large percentage of abortions performed before the twelfth week of gestation.

Dilation and Curettage (D & C)

Like suction aspiration, D & C is employable during the first trimester of pregnancy. The technique is similar, too, commencing with the instrumental expansion of the cervical opening. After dilation is sufficiently accomplished, a curette, or loop-shaped steel knife, is inserted into the uterus and is used to sever the baby and placenta. Amid bleeding which is usually quite profuse, the womb contents are manually scraped out into a bucket or basin. Often, this procedure is applied in conjunction with the suction method. Like the suction method, it is used for first trimester abortions (within the first three months of the pregnancy).

Saline Injection

Saline is the preferred method of abortion for pregnancies that have advanced into the second trimester of the pregnancy (the fourth, fifth, and sixth months since conception). This procedure, sometimes called ''salting out,'' is most reliable beyond the fifteenth week when the amniotic sac has reached an adequate size.

First, a large needle is inserted into the amnion through the abdominal wall of the mother just below her navel. Approximately four ounces of fluid are withdrawn through the needle and replaced with six ounces of a very strong saline solution. (Occasionally a 50% glucose solution is substituted.) The child breathes and swallows this life-sapping fluid. Slow and painful is the little one's death. He or she may struggle, hemorrhage, and convulse for an hour or more before dying. The corrosive properties of the salt concentration may burn away the delicate outer layer of the child's skin, exposing the red subcutaneous tissue. This excoriation produces the dark, almost glossy appearance characteristic of the saline baby. On rare occasion, a child may escape death despite the lethal injection of saline and emerge from the birth canal seared but very much alive.

Dilation and Evacuation (D & E)

The discomfort of an induced labor, the risk of misplaced saline, and the trauma of giving birth to a seared but alive infant have created many foes of the saline technique. Increasingly, a modified version of the D & C is becoming available to the woman seeking a late abortion.

The procedure, known as dilation and evacuation, or D & E, is not universally practiced or even accepted by purveyors of mid-trimester abortions. The size of the child and the extent of his or her development make this method time-consuming and quite distasteful.

The technique, like the D & C, begins with the forcible dilation of the cervix. By "feel" the physician then uses the curette to lacerate and dismember the baby and chop the surrounding vessels and tissues. Emptying the uterus is tricky. Although suction may be helpful, the large, uncrushable parts of the child's body must be carefully guided out through the birth canal with the aid of forceps.

To avert the possibility of infection, the physician may fit the fetal pieces back together like a puzzle. This reassemblage will reveal any "missing" portions of the body and thus the need for further evacuative measures.

Prostaglandin Abortion

Prostaglandins occur naturally in many tissues of the human body. Their functions range from affecting heart rate and blood pressure to influencing intestinal activity. However, it is their ability to stimulate contractions of the uterus that has prompted their use as an abortifacient.

An administration of prostaglandins induces uterine contractions and begins labor. Because this technique instigates the natural birth process, it can be used during virtually any stage of pregnancy.

Prostaglandins cause constriction of fetal blood vessels and disrupt proper functioning of the heart. Death may be very slow in coming. The child may suffer as if having a "heart attack" for up to 48 hours.

A chemically induced abortion might seem to be the "ideal," affording the least intrusive course back to a non-pregnant state. Yet, the use of prostaglandins is not without certain risks. Along with the unpleasant side effects of vomiting and fever, incomplete emptying of the uterus can lead to infection or the need for a surgical procedure to accomplish total evacuation.

In addition, the odds of delivering a child that can endure the effects of prostaglandins and the stress of labor increase as a pregnancy progresses.

Hysterotomy

A "mini" Caesarean section, the hysterotomy is performed in late pregnancy when the instillation of saline failed to expel the child or was inadvisable for medical reasons. The mother's abdomen and uterus are surgically opened and the baby is lifted out of her body. When the umbilical cord is clamped, death may be immediate or the child may struggle for several minutes before succumbing.

Reportedly, there are a number of children alive today who are products of "unsuccessful" hysterotomies. Perhaps this is the most feared "complication" of this type of abortion. Live births can be quite distressful for patient and staff alike. To preclude the "hardship" of such a birth, a dose of saline may be given prior to surgery to insure the demise of the child.

The following chart shows abortion percentages by week of gestation:

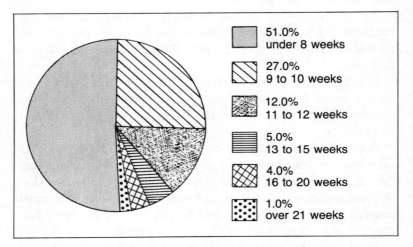

51.0%
under 8 weeks

27.0%
9 to 10 weeks

12.0%
11 to 12 weeks

5.0%
13 to 15 weeks

4.0%
16 to 20 weeks

1.0%
over 21 weeks

(Remember, even though only 1% of all abortions occur beyond the 21st week, that still means nearly 40 per day!)

Many women have spoken of their "positive" experiences in abortion clinics. They were fortunate enough to have come upon kind and helpful staff and to undergo quick and uncomplicated procedures. The darkest extreme, however, seems to have found its way into many pieces of staunch anti-abortion writings.

And, yes, many of us have seen the nauseating photographs of abortuses stockpiled in barrels or garbage cans.

We've revolted at the thought of blood-thirsty doctors enticed by the lucrative profits in the business of abortion. The demand for abortion, especially in metropolitan areas, sometimes creates gross over-scheduling in clinics and hospitals. The procedures must be done in such rapid sequence that many women complain of being shuffled about like cattle. The "success" of a day's work is often measured by the number of completed operations. In such clinics women are processed in an almost assembly line-like fashion. In the interest of expediency, a doctor may work out of two operating rooms so one woman can be prepared while another is aborted. He shuttles between the rooms and, if all goes smoothly, may boast a rate of six, seven, or even eight completed abortions per hour.

We've winced our way through the classical circulation of horror stories about abortion clinics: women who are injected with saline and left to deliver their babies alone or with numbed medical personnel; nurses who have found patients cradling their aborted children; "failed" procedures which have yielded babies struggling to breathe, some of whom refuse to die on their own; doctors using a towel, hand, or placenta to "finish" the job; bags of fetal remains left in trash bins; abortuses being stored in formaldehyde awaiting experimentation.

These reports are deeply troubling, to say the least. Still, I'm not convinced that such happenings are commonplace despite the propensity of many pro-life authors to sensationalize accounts of this nature. And although I count myself among their ranks, I believe the weighty moral considerations against abortion are sufficient to stand on their own.

I will concede, however, that the grisly tales of conduct in abortion mills and the pitiful photographs of trashed babies are persuasive in their own way and I can agree that the fact that such incidents take place at all, however infrequently, only seems to compound the iniquity of abortion.

Yet it isn't enough to be repulsed by the physical realities. One might squirm uncomfortably at the sight of open-heart surgery without finding it morally offensive. Even if it was possible to eliminate the "gore," would it be enough? If it was within our power to devise a totally pain-free abortifacient (for mother and child), would abortion itself somehow become more palatable?

If we were satisfied that abortion was only an act of medicine, it might be sufficient to simply "clean up" its modes and venues. But a mere clinical procedure it is not. Regardless of the type of abortion employed, and regardless of the demeanor of the facility and its personnel and the degree of "respect" displayed toward patient and fetus, regardless of their methods of disposing of fetal remains and their policy concerning live births, the end result is unchanged. Babies are killed. And whitewashing that isn't possible.

Abortion, even under the "best" of conditions, leaves behind an ugly trail of unresolved moral concerns. It is to these questions of morality that we next direct our attention.

Death Plans

I have an unplanned pregnancy
What a crying shame!
I'll have to plan a death
To stay ahead of the game.

"Let's see, there's an opening
Tuesday at eight
We have a tight schedule
Please don't be late."

"I have a class that day
How 'bout Wednesday at ten?"
"Yes, we can squeeze you in;
OK, we'll see you then."

Now you have but hours
My precious little one
Your death has been planned
Though life's barely begun.

CHAPTER THREE

Deceptive Claims
of the
Pro-Abortionists

The phone rang one evening about a week prior to a national election. It was a woman calling from a locally based campaign headquarters with a pitch for her party's candidate — could she count on my vote? I thanked her for calling but explained I had decided to support another candidate.

"May I ask why?" came the voice.

"Among other things I admire his pro-life position," I replied.

With audible indignation she countered, "Well, I've always thought a woman should have control of her own body."

"Excuse me," I said politely, "didn't you call to ask me for my opinion?"

It is clear that the abortion issue is unsurpassed in its ability to generate controversy. Few topics of conversation can so quickly turn to an emotionally charged volley of opinion. Nearly everyone has strong feelings about abortion — in one direction or the other.

The friends of abortion rejoice in the new legal recognition of what they consider to be a basic right. Many feel threatened by the open resistance of the pro-life movement.

Its foes, on the other hand, find it impossible to see abortion as anything other than an act of murder. The legal position is regarded as an intolerable approval of the slaughter of innocents.

One thing is certain. The issue wasn't "settled" in 1973. The abortion debate continues in full force, even well into the second decade of legalization.

From this heated exchange, do any real answers emerge?

This chapter shall devote itself to close examination of the claims that brought to being, and which now defend, a policy of abortion-on-demand. In it I will lay siege, one by one, to the array of arguments voiced most often by the pro-abortion forces. This shan't be a task of great difficulty. Although the assertions sport a superficial appeal, they cannot withstand the scrutiny of an honest and forthright evaluation.

A Woman's Body Is Her Own

With the national spotlight trained on the issue of women's rights, such a claim seems to fit neatly into the ideal concept of social equality. Who would deny a woman (or any person) the right to exercise complete control over her own body? Surely such authority is of primal importance among all other rights. However, as a rationale for the right to an abortion, the philosophy of this argument is revealed to be specious to the point of self-contradiction.

First, no one has absolute control over his or her own body — either in the eyes of God or in the principles of secular law. For example, suicide and prostitution are both expressly forbidden. It is considered wrong to use illicit drugs or to engage in any self-abusive activity. We are taught that our bodies are sacred and rights to any self-induced maltreatment are nonexistent in both legal and Christian doctrine.

"Do you not know that your body is a temple of the holy Spirit within you, whom you have from God, and that you are not your own? For you have been purchased at a price. Therefore glorify God in your body" (1 Corinthians 6:19-20).

Further, no one possesses the license to encroach upon another's rights. The rights of an individual at any given time or circumstance hinge largely on those around him or her. There are no absolutes in a community that has more than one member. Individual liberty must be circumscribed to the interest and needs of the whole. For instance, anyone with a valid driver's license has the right to drive his or her car down the highway. However, should someone be standing in the middle of the road, such a right immediately becomes void. Violation of another's life, or at best, that person's well-being, invalidates the lesser right to drive on a particular roadway.

A person on trial for driving under the influence of drugs or alcohol would find a useless defense in the "freedom to do what I want with my own body" argument. An intoxicated driver is obviously a hazard to other drivers or pedestrians on the road. Their rights of protection of life and limb clearly overrule any rights the indicted person claims for his or her own body.

Secondly, biological data have rendered the undeniable conclusion that a separate life is begun at the meeting of sperm and egg. The product of conception is a human being with a body distinct from his or her mother, often in such elemental attributes as blood type and sex. So, any choices or decisions made regarding an established pregnancy do involve another person, however hidden, however forsaken. Those who harbor doubt need only consider the advancements that have led to test tube babies and embryo transfers. From this laboratory procedure one fact establishes itself: The tiniest baby in his or her most delicate state can exist and develop outside the abode of the natural mother. (The crucial matter of fetal life shall receive a more complete evaluation in the following section.)

I move on to my third point at the risk of appearing hopelessly Victorian. The case of rape aside, the woman is not the victim in an unwanted pregnancy. Motherhood is not cast upon her like a spell from the blue. Has she not already made a choice? In the vast majority of cases the answer is yes — she has exercised her right to "freedom of choice" by choosing to have sex, by choosing to make herself susceptible to pregnancy. And although it may not be what she wanted or intended, she should have been aware that conception is an inherent possibility of such a choice.

Each time a driver gets behind the wheel of a vehicle he or she runs the risk, however slight, of being killed in an accident. Precautionary measures such as seat belts and moderate speeds will only reduce the chances of becoming a traffic fatality. The only guarantee of not being killed in an auto accident is to stay out of autos!

This is not a plea for celibacy nor is it an attempt to liken pregnancy with the casualties of vehicular mishaps. The point it serves is a simple one. Choices involve consequences. Pregnancy, among other things, is a possible consequence of a sexual encounter.

Choices are made every day. Involved in these continual decision-making processes — from eating a candy bar to parachuting from a plane — are considerations of effect and outcome, of consequence and risk. Honesty prompts us to acknowledge that abortion is not a valid alternative at all, but a bleak attempt to eradicate the consequence of an earlier choice.

If such an allegation appears to be anti-feministic hoopla, I can only offer a gentle reminder that it is put forth in the interest of the 750,000 females (and the same number of males) who meet their death through abortion each year in the United States. Where is their freedom of choice?

If a single word is at the center of controversy here, that word is "freedom." Abortion advocates contend that a woman's personal "freedom" is compromised unforgivably when her reproductive choices do not include abortion.

Just what is freedom? Perhaps a more perceptive understanding will emerge from a discussion of what freedom is not.

Freedom is not free-reign. (What society would be free if its citizens were allowed to run amuck and indulge their every whim? For these individuals, such impulsive self-gratification could not possibly be equated with freedom.)

It is not a carefree state incurred by the accumulation of privileges and the elimination of restrictions.

Nor is it an end to be realized to the neglect and sacrifice of all else.

Rather, freedom is a state that grows from an awareness and acceptance of the truth.

"You will know the truth, and the truth will set you free" (John 8:32).

If the option of killing her child must avail itself before a woman can possess unconditional equality, it is a shallow freedom indeed. What kind of "freedom" is found when the oppression she seeks to avoid is turned on her own son or daughter? What liberation exists in deserting the biological reality that the child inside is alive and human? In short, in deserting the truth? In this way she has become a self-made slave to her own fertility.

Even the freest nation in the world has a sophisticated network of laws and statutes, and the freest individuals I know live along moral guidelines as well as legal ones. The interrelationship of civic freedoms and moral, or individual, freedoms is a tangent point of controversy and is outside the scope of this writing. Let it suffice to note that discipline, responsibility, and prudence are the great forerunners of freedom at any echelon.

Despite an ongoing eagerness to interchange the terms "freedom to choose" and "right to choose" in the abortion debate, a brief point of distinction is in order. Certainly freedom — in the sense of free will — exists for everyone. We are "free" to do just about anything, including the perpetration of such acts of violence and destruction as stealing, vandalizing, even murdering. In contrast, rights, with a more prescriptive connotation, involve legal and moral privileges set in accordance with accepted standards of proper behavior. So, it may be said, that our aforementioned motorist, while having the freedom to run down a person on the road, obviously hasn't the right to such an act.

Therefore, in the abortion controversy, it is not so much the "freedom" to choose which is in question but rather the "right" to choose. As previously indicated, the rights of one individual cannot encroach upon the rights of neighboring individuals. One's rights are workable only in the broader context of the rights of all. The moment we speak of quashing the rights of a group, or of even one, as a triumph for the general cause of freedom, at that very instant we cede the stuff of true freedom for a cheap imitation.

In summary, to justify abortion on the merits of the introductory argument is to disregard three fundamental truths: Rights to our own bodies are not absolute, particularly when others are affected by our actions and choices; a fetus is not an extension of his or her mother's body. The baby is biologically in her, not of her; pregnancy is a sequential result of a given act — the prerogative of abortion decries the antecedent choice, the real choice, of engaging in sexual intercourse.

To address the claims of a feverish, abortion-happy crusade to insure "equal rights" and "freedom of choice" to all women, one needs only embrace the logic of the movement and carry it to term. Social equality and the freedom to choose are wonderful provisions. But, by their own standards, they must enjoy a universal application if they are to have any meaning at all.

It's Only a Cluster of Cells

The devastating earthquake Mexico suffered in 1985 left thousands dead and much of its capital city in ruins. For days and weeks after the tragedy workers and volunteers frantically searched the debris for survivors. Beneath tons of concrete rubble many were found alive, including a number of newborn infants who had endured days without food or water.

A few years ago an avalanche at a ski resort in the Sierras buried several people. After all but one of the bodies had been found and removed by a crew of workers, there was little hope that the remaining victim, a woman, would be discovered alive. Still the rescue team proceeded quickly and cautiously (so as not to further jeopardize her safety and well-being), always working under the hope — indeed, the assumption — that she was alive. Happily, even after days of freezing temperatures, she was.

Such is the way of the civilized human condition. In matters of life and death there is an unwritten law that assigns the burden of proof to determining the absence of life. Life itself is privileged the benefit of the doubt, even if that doubt seems insuperable. In a hospital, at the scene of an accident or natural disaster, in any emergency situation, the presence of life is presupposed. Non-life or death must be categorically proven.

Enter legal abortion. Should the unborn have to "prove" they are alive to win the acceptance and protection of society? Such a state of affairs, in blatant conflict with traditional policy, was brought about by the pro-abortion movement. Disregarding the most crucial matter of fetal status or fetal life, its attention is given, rather, to the extraneous circumstances of those living outside the womb. Arguments in support of abortion plead for the well-being, comfort, and convenience of the mother who is "already here." Is there any concern on the part of abortion proponents that the babies being extinguished might be alive? Perhaps some. Yet I find it puzzling that they rarely tackle this point directly. Many supporters of abortion distance themselves from biological data using depersonalizing terminology such as "blob of protoplasm" or "product of conception" in their references to the unborn.

After conception, something is present that wasn't before. Whether it is a tiny human being or a purposeless "blob" is not a question to be swept under the rug. So much is at stake. So much depends upon the answer. Indeed, this single revelation is central to the whole issue of abortion. The nature and status of the conceptus bear overridingly on the implications of the abortion act, marking the difference between a procedure to remove a growth and an incidence of murder.

Although fetal development has been traversed in some detail, let us review the accomplished growth at six weeks gestation which is a usual time for a pregnancy to be confirmed. At this stage, our "blob" has sprouted arms and legs and it has an unmistakably human face. All of its major organs are nearly complete and already working! Its heart is beating and its brain shows measurable activity. By its own power this "mass of tissue" has secured a source of nourishment for itself. In light of this, can we truthfully call it a random grouping of cells? Hardly.

The very definition of life (Random House) seems to have been written for and about prenatal existence: "the condition that distinguishes animals and plants from inorganic objects and dead organisms, being manifested by growth through metabolism, reproduction, and the power of adaption to environment through changes originating internally."

We hear much in the way of "potential" life. Supporters of abortion argue that the product of conception is but a "potential" human being in the way a seed is a "potential" flower. To compare people and plants may be distracting, but if it sheds new light on an area that may be shadowy for some, it is well worth a momentary digression.

Let us think of a seed as a plant in its earliest form. It must advance through various stages of growth before flowering, yet it always remains the same plant. The first form of the human body, the zygote, will successively develop into newborn, toddler, child, teenager, and, finally, adult. Yet the same person abides throughout the days, weeks, months, and years of growth and change.

To declare that a fetus is not a baby is like saying a baby is not a teenager. The argument lacks the vision of the common thread that links all levels of development — humanness. For the zygote could be nothing else but human and could produce nothing else but a human baby which, in turn, could become nothing else but a human child and so on — just as a particular seed can yield only a specific type of flower or fruit or vegetable.

From another angle, if it is correct to say that a zygote is only a potential baby, is it not also correct to aver that a zygote is a potential doctor, lawyer, or bus driver? The key difference is that the latter represents only possibilities and "maybe somedays" while the former denotes something that will take place — an inevitable event, barring death, that will come to pass.

The term "potential" human life is incorrectly applied to the zygote and fetus for it implies only possibilities, not actualities. The zygote is not something that will one day be capable of life. It is bursting with energy, alive and growing immediately upon its origination at fertilization. Its life is an actuality.

You were once a zygote. So was I. Our parents and grandparents began life as zygotes, too. So did Thomas Jefferson, Louis Pasteur, and the jogger in the park. It is both sad and true that some human beings, through a variety of causes, such as improper implantation and spontaneous or induced abortions, lose their lives before they have a chance to completely develop. Yet these little ones are no less human than the rest of us. Less mature, yes. But not less human.

One doesn't gradually and obscurely "come to life" as his or her physical development progresses. If such were the case, a person would be nearly two decades old before being completely "alive" and human. Full humanness is present at the starting gate of earthly life, conception.

Those who search out a point of transition during prenatal development that marks the onset of "life" or "humanness" do so arbitrarily and often under the influence of an ulterior desire to be free of the fetus or to support others in freeing themselves. There is no magic moment at which time the "blob" is transformed into a baby — no magic number of cells (100? 1,000? 1,000,000?) that distinguishes a mass of proteins and tissues from a human body. From conception until natural death, the vital continuum of existence is so powerful and so purposeful that no scientific distinction can be had between the life of the unborn, the newly born, and the fully matured adult.

Thus the term "meaningful life" was born into the arena of pro-abortion jargon. What a misplanted term! What, exactly, is meaningful life? And who decides? Does a drunk in an alley have meaningful life? Or a comatose accident victim? Not by the standards of some, maybe, yet it would be immoral and illegal to kill either one. Can one fetus have meaningful life and not another? It seems "meaningful life," as used in the abortion debate, is a cowardly, meaningless phrase.

The intentions of God are apparent in the many biblical allusions to the unborn. He relates to people individually, post-conception and even pre-conception, and always in an intimate, knowing way. The teachings of the Bible reveal God to be the Creator of each person with a specific goal in mind, a certain purpose to be brought to fulfillment by a called follower. In this sacred doctrine, as in the documentations of the science of embryology, there is no room for talk of "potential" life or life without "meaning." All indicators beckon us to the realization that the unborn being is a vital biological and spiritual entity — alive in every sense of the word.[1]

Children in the Way

The hearts that beat so grandly
    are forever stilled
Blood that flows so freely
    is carelessly spilled
The tiny warm and growing bodies
    are eerily chilled
The new destinies, the budding futures
    prematurely filled
Not by God's ultimate wisdom
    but by man willed
Children in the way
    are quietly killed.

Every Child Should Be Wanted

Child rearing is an awesome responsibility. Many pregnancies begin with a certain amount of apprehension, anxiety, and, for some, even despair. Perhaps pregnancy is an even more volatile state for the unmarried or financially encumbered or for those who are deeply involved in career goals or raising other children. Happily, the majority who do experience negative emotions in early pregnancy find they are fleeting. Many obstetricians will affirm that very often these unpleasant feelings will fade and give way to the full impact of the loving maternal instinct. Most all babies who were "unplanned" or "unwanted" come to be loved very much. Mothers of both "wanted" and initially "unwanted" children usually can admit to no difference in the degree of love they feel for each of their offspring.[2]

To one with doubts or misgivings early on in pregnancy, abortion only seems an easy way out. Surely many children who have lost their lives under these circumstances would have been, one day, dearly cherished.

Despite all of this, I would be amiss not to acknowledge that some women truly do not want their unborn children. The "unwanted" child is a term used so often it has become a mainstay in the vocabulary of pro-abortion groups. "Let there be no unwanted children!" "Every child deserves to be wanted!" Such ingratiatory slogans! For although the word "unwanted" might have some use for describing "things" it is, in this case, a misleading adjective for it reveals an aspect of the person doing the unwanting, not the unwanted object. To describe a particular child, one might note that he has blond hair, green eyes, or his daddy's nose — but what does "unwanted" tell us about him? Nothing. The term is a reflection of those around the baby, an indication of how they view and respond to his presence. The baby is not the source but rather the object of this attitude. For while a child can't simultaneously be both tall and short or have both brown eyes and blue eyes, he can be concurrently "unwanted" by his mother and very "wanted" by someone else, perhaps another relative or one of the thousands of childless couples across our country. There are no unwanted children, only unwanting parents.

This tangle of wants and don't-wants can be reduced to how a person perceives a specific object in one's future. The same perceptions which might prompt one to want a new pair of shoes or a Hawaiian vacation direct one's feelings about unborn children, for they, too, are yet unseen, unexperienced by those around them. Not able to exact responses and reactions based on their qualities as individuals, all existing perceptions of them originate in the minds and hearts of their families. On this they are tried, judged, and sentenced.

When our court system ruled in favor of abortion on demand, suddenly this huge variant of individual perception arose as the unborn child's legal measure of worth. The convenience of his or her family members and their inclination to make allowances or sacrifices for the child became a life and death barometer.

Surely each one of us has encountered the feeling of being isolated, misunderstood, or unwanted at some point. Many, if not all, parents have experienced on occasion times when born children were annoying, disappointing, maybe even temporarily "unwanted." What a beautiful and harmonious world would be ours if every child was always wanted by his parents, and, conversely, if every parent was unceasingly wanted by his or her children — spouse wanted by spouse, brother by brother, friend by friend.

Meanwhile, until this Utopian state becomes a reality, the true index of our Christian disposition is disclosed in how we deal with those found to be "undesirable." Do we shun them? Persecute them? Murder them?

The concept of eliminating undesirables from society would seem too preposterous to entertain. If in being unwanted and unaccepted one was earmarked for death, then surely each one of us would live in a constant state of jeopardy, particularly members of minority groups, the aged and infirm, the homeless and handicapped. Further, the ethical postulates of selective expurgation are vast. What reasonable person would condone the prescribed killing of someone considered undesirable by a community or, worse yet, by a particular individual? Yet, continually the unborn are involved in a deadly competition they don't even know exists. They must "measure up" to the wants and wishes of others or fall victims to a somber end.

Is it fair that two children who are equal in every way can be subject to such radically different fates because of the wishes of those around them? Is it fair to gauge any one human being by the perceptions of another? I learned long ago that the abortion issue has nothing to do with fairness — only unqualified selfishness. Sometimes this selfishness wears the hat of humanitarianism or compassion, as in the argument that it isn't right for a child to be born to unwilling parents.

But, let's not allow this train of logic to end here. No one would deny that ideally each child should be welcomed and wanted. But what of those who aren't? Since they already exist, the price tag for the "every child a wanted child" condition is their induced deaths. Should the slogans instead read: "Every child should be wanted — or killed" or "No unwanted child should live" or "Abortion is mercy killing for the unborn"? These are the unwritten, unspoken messages behind the campaign to make sure only "wanted" children see the light of day. Can we actually believe death to be a merciful alternative? If so, we are operating under the reckless presumption that a potentially happy extra-uterine existence awaits only the child of a wanting parent and that all others are better off with no life at all. Obviously, there are no guarantees for anyone, even the very wanted.

If we are truly plagued by the uncertain lots that await unwanted children, we would do well to remember that almighty God assigns no problem or dilemma without the grace, strength, and means to handle it. We must seek his help and pursue his guidance for solutions. We have to know that ending the lives of our unseen sons and daughters is not the answer.

Abortion Checks Overpopulation and World Hunger

With many nations packing heavy concentrations of people into relatively small areas, the population density of the United States remains surprisingly low, with an average of only about 70 inhabitants per square mile. In fact, for every American man, woman, and child there is a full acre of land in the combined areas of Texas and New Mexico alone! And although the nation's birth rate has dropped from its "Baby Boom" levels, the business of agriculture continues to expand. The U.S., which comprises only a tiny percentage of the globe's population, outpaces all other nations in food production. The truth is, there is no shortage of room or resources to accommodate the current population and even one much greater.

Then what about our fellow countrymen who live on the streets? And those without enough food? Poverty is a way of life for a shameful number of Americans. The above facts do little to fill their stomachs or shelter them from the rain.

When there are hungry and homeless among us, it is time to address the internal disorders which have spawned such a situation in one of the richest of all the world's nations.

On a vaster scale, a goodly portion of the world's people lives in a constant state of hunger and deprivation. Some argue that more children to feed here means less food for the starving over there and that eliminating these extra mouths for the purpose of population control is perfectly justified.[3]

The idea of decimating the population is not without serious implications. Thinning large numbers of people by the systematic murders of selected groups of born citizens is morally unthinkable. Who could tolerate the mandated killing of everyone over a designated age? Or of the "unproductive" sectors of the populus such as the poor or disabled who eat but don't "contribute"? For many, however, antipathy shifts to acceptance when unseen, unborn children are the chosen lot.

Yet, I suspect precious few abortions are performed for reasons of overpopulation and widespread starvation. Certainly, the multitudes of happily pregnant women are not besieged by appeals to abort nor are they made to feel that they are committing a terrible injustice against their country or the hungry people of the world by having their babies. Conversely, how many women have undergone abortions and then donated to the poor the thousands of dollars that would have been spent on food for the child? If the answer is none, how do the starving profit by abortion?

The practice of abortion has been around for some time. Never has there been, nor is it likely there ever will be, any indication that jettisoning the unborn reduces the number of hungry at home or abroad. Instead, the notion of killing babies for lack of food clashes head on with the relatively opulent lifestyles so often found in the U.S.

First, it is estimated Americans throw away a full 15% of their food! Our waste in a year could feed every citizen of a Third World country quite well for that same twelve-month period of time.

Secondly, recent surveys indicate that a third of all Americans is overweight. Using a modest estimate of ten pounds of excess weight for each of these people, we have the caloric equivalent of more than one billion gallons of whole milk or about the same amount of steamed rice. Staggering? Yes.

Lavish spending is another point of incongruity. When billions of dollars are spent annually on everything from jewels and furs to greeting cards and gift wrap while life is denied to the world's newest occupants because there is "not enough," something is terribly wrong. How is it that someone so concerned about world hunger can squander $50 on a steak dinner when that amount could easily buy a month's food for a family in a poverty-stricken country?

Protracted world hunger is a grave and complicated predicament, and one that precludes the possibility of a simple or instantaneous remedy. But one thing is certain. Having babies does not take food out of the mouths of the hungry nor is killing babies the answer to large-scale famine. Let us not place blame on the blameless. Let us not encumber the unborn with the monumental problems of overcrowding and mass starvation. A far more sensible, effective, and humane search for a solution might begin with attempts to equalize the world situation a bit — to curb some of the indulgence and to reduce the waste and prodigal expenditures both on national and personal levels.

Ours is a large and fruitful planet. It can yield food enough for many times its current number of inhabitants. There is no rhyme or reason in using abortion as a weapon against hunger.

No Child of Rape Should Live

Rape. Incest. Such acts of violence and degradation, such willful abuse of another's body can provoke in the victim feelings of rage, terror, frustration, and helplessness to extremes beyond the apprehensions of anyone who has not experienced these violent crimes. Complicate this with a resulting pregnancy and the situation could seem intolerable. That such barbarism could occur without the chance of proper legal restitution for the victim may appear unthinkably cruel. Surely, it is a heartless society that would refuse her an abortion.

The ordeal of rape is like no other. That is why it is imperative to remain ever mindful of and ever sensitive to the woman and her needs while exploring the morality of abortion after a sexual violation. (Hereafter, for the purposes of this writing, all such transgressions will be included in the context of rape.)

Thankfully, even though the instance of rape is one of the most frequently cited arguments in support of legal abortion, rape-induced pregnancies are extremely rare. Yet, when one does occur, society has supplied an almost pre-charted course of action — interruption of that pregnancy. Abortion after a fecund rape has become standardized procedure. Yet, in any situation attended by moral concerns, a comprehensive analysis is essential. A one-sided morality begs us destroy the fruit of a dehumanizing, immoral union. But an all-encompassing morality, even under these, the most heinous of all conditions, won't allow overlooking the child.

The circumstances surrounding the sexual act have no bearing on the value of the child that might be created. A person is a person. A life is a life. And as revolting as the act of rape is, it cannot be considered the moral co-equal of life. Only life itself is ethically comparable to life. Therefore a sexual violation cannot possibly justify a death, particularly the death of one completely devoid of any criminal intention.[4]

What a gruesome paradox was created with the injection of abortion into society's system of dispensing justice — that a child might be punished for his or her father's offense.

But what about the victimized woman? Wouldn't carrying a child after being forcibly, brutally impregnated only compound the trauma of rape?

This is a question without easy answers. Varying circumstances and personalities make it impossible to determine an all-purpose solution to the dilemma of a pregnancy brought about by violence. Yet the propriety of killing her own, albeit ill-gotten, child is indeed debatable and may not best serve the needs of the victim at all.

Too often the possible positive psychological benefits of completing the pregnancy are overlooked in the haste for instant redress after rape. After being invaded so viciously, the victim of rape may want nothing more than to forget the entire experience. But, the trouble is, once the emotional damage has occurred nothing she can do will erase the effects of the episode from her mind. So, should she respond by doing something equally destructive and violently unnatural? What beneficent effect could this have — to know she has violated another's body in a way not all that unsimilar to the attack on her own? Has she not herself been wrongfully victimized by the overpowering brute strength of another?

When a woman is forced to live with the excruciating memories of a rape and subsequent pregnancy, there may be some degree of comfort in being able to remember giving life rather than destroying it. If mitigation of such pain and humiliation is possible, perhaps it is only through an unselfish response to such a frightful predicament. A positive attitude and course of conduct can only propagate positive results. Of course bearing a child under these circumstances is difficult at best. Sensitive counseling and loving support are of paramount importance throughout the duration of the pregnancy and afterward in meeting and dealing with the alternatives that present themselves.

Rape is a bestial offense. But sometimes the atrocity of the crime and the emotional turmoil it ignites can belie the divine creation it may effect. We must remember that there is already one unfortunate victim after rape. Why needlessly make it two?

Preserve the Mother's Health at All Costs

This statement bristles with many medical, legal, and moral implications. What constitutes ''danger'' or ''risk'' to the mother? How operative can vague legal jargon be to a doctor who must work with individual patients and sets of circumstances? And, finally, can doctors, lawmakers, or family members rightfully and in good conscience choose to end one life because it may pose a threat to another?

The answers are not simple. From a medical standpoint, there is a ''risk'' in any pregnancy, albeit far less than 1% for normal, healthy women. The danger in carrying a child to term increases with certain conditions of the mother such as diabetes, advanced age, obesity, a history of heart ailments, blood clots, or respiratory problems, to name a few. As the risk factor climbs, is there an acceptable point, statistically, that justifies ending a child's life? If so, what is that point? And who decides?

Legalities regarding the application of abortion in ''risky'' pregnancies are of little use. Lawmakers haven't the expertise of their medical counterparts and, given that doctors must treat a full range of situations from the mildly serious to the critical, legal regulations can't possibly prescribe a single, well-defined policy for medical professionals to follow. Hence, in that area of the abortion issue where the medical and legal domains overlap, legislative explications are sketchy and inconclusive. Often, legal guidelines lack exactness of wording, leaving their interpretations to the subjective discretion of the attending physician.

For instance, any individual situation pertaining to abortion could secure a legal foothold in phraseology like: "Maternity or additional offspring may force upon the woman a distressful life and future. Psychological harm may be imminent. Mental and physical health may be taxed by child care. There is also the distress for all concerned associated with the unwanted child, and there is the problem of bringing a child into a family already unable, psychologically or otherwise, to care for it. In other cases the additional difficulties . . . of unwed motherhood may be involved. All these are factors that the woman and the responsible physician will consider in consultation."[5]

Medically speaking, the risk in a pregnancy may be "measured" using an evaluation of the patient's history and a statistical assessment of her condition. And while these criteria can be helpful and afford some degree of accuracy to a prognosis, they fall within the limited scope of medical prescience and cannot be considered absolutes. Doctors are human and their medical training is not infallible nor does it lend them divine judgment or foresight to share with their patients.

Far above the murky waters of legal terminology and beyond the wanton reliability of statistics and the projections of doctors resides morality. From this vantage, we must ask, is abortion ever morally warranted in a pregnancy that threatens the health of a woman? What, if any, statistical risk factor (1%, 5%, 10%?) converts the termination of a pregnancy from an unacceptable act to one that is morally sanctioned?

The answers are secured in the solidity of this understanding: Morality is an absolute, rooted in a whole and perfect love. It transcends the capacities of educated guesswork or licensed speculation. In short, morality cannot yield to non-absolutes. Therefore, the intentional killing of a child, even in a precarious medical contingency, is a grave moral iniquity.

I hasten to add that this sentiment isn't suggesting doctors sit by and watch a woman die of the complications of a pregnancy or of a chronic illness or condition aggravated by the child she is carrying. On the contrary, if her life appears to be in immediate danger, a competent physician will make every attempt to save her. If these measures result in death for her baby it is tragic, however not as tragic as would be the loss of both mother and child. The death of a baby as a consequence of efforts to save the mother is diametrically opposed to the notion of automatically aborting the baby along the due course of medical proceedings just because he or she may represent a calculated risk.

Happily, the need for true "therapeutic" abortions is almost nonexistent. Life-threatening pregnancies occur very infrequently and, at those times, the care of a qualified physician can usually bring both mother and baby safely to term. In fact, fewer than one pregnancy in 6,000 will result in death for the mother. Yet this statistic is grossly misrepresented by the fact that each year hundreds of thousands of abortions take place to spare the "health" of the mother.

The "emotional" risks of pregnancy have received an unprecedented amount of attention of late. It is argued that an unwanted pregnancy can be devastating to a woman in a fragile psychological state. Interesting to note is that pregnant women in general are found to be in healthier emotional form than non-pregnant women. Suicide rates drop to a level far below normal in women carrying children.

Clearly, an unhappily pregnant woman can be distraught over her situation, but if abortion was permitted only when an actual mental breakdown threatened, how rarely it would be used! Even then, can we weigh the psychological hardships of a pregnancy against the life of a child?

In the abortion arena, "health" has become an elastic word, stretching easily to meet a diverse assortment of needs. As intimated in the excerpt by the Supreme Court earlier in this section, the term is construed to encompass a woman's physical, emotional, even familial and financial satisfaction and well-being. Once again, this imprecise handling of language creates a catch-all into which any level of mental discomfort, hardship, or frustration can be deposited. For all intents and purposes, abortion for "health," under the court's working definition, is abortion on demand.

The conclusion is twofold. First, the specious argument for abortion to protect the mother has been fervently misused. So much of what passes for concern for maternal safety, particularly in late pregnancy, is no more than the erection of a safe passage to permissible abortion. A distressingly large number of children are put to death each year under the rubric of "saving the mother's life."

Secondly, medical statistics and risk factors, with their margins of error and susceptibility to misinterpretation, are nonabsolute guidelines and can find no welcome in a morality that places a premium on life. For what is absolutely certain is that two lives are involved in a pregnancy — each deserving consideration, respect, and the full advantages of modern medical knowledge and application.

Abortion Prevents Child Abuse

Time and time again we've heard that legalized abortion reduces the number of battered and abused children. This claim is used unhaltingly by pro-abortion forces despite lack of evidence to support it.

What statistics do maintain is that child abuse has been on the rise in this country since the advent of legalized abortion — up nearly 400% since 1973![6]

Other recent studies are working to dispel the myth that legal abortion curtails the acrimonious or hostile treatment of young children. Indeed, there is now speculation in the opposite direction — that increased rates of abortion may actually incubate a social climate ripe for other abuses of the young and helpless.[7]

It is easy enough to make flashy generalities about unwantedness and battered children, but it has been shown that the products of these "unwanted" pregnancies are no more likely to be mistreated by their parents than are children of planned or very wanted pregnancies. Not all, and not even many, parents of unplanned children are predisposed to violence. Rather, studies reveal that abusive behavioral tendencies in adults frequently have roots that can be traced back to their own childhoods.[8]

Thus, the offspring of parents who were themselves victimized as youngsters may be the most likely targets of abuse regardless of parental attitudes during pregnancy. The initial feelings toward a child do not portend the manner in which he or she will be accepted, loved, or raised after the birth takes place.

To forecast future violation of children and to accept the solution of abortion for the ''good'' of potential victims is more than just absurd, it is screamingly unfair. First, because the intense emotions of pregnancy are often quite temporary; and secondly because it has been statistically established that the fuel which drives child abusers does not flow from the predicament of an unwanted pregnancy.

For, even in the absence of these corroborating statistics and sociological discoveries about familial patterns of neglect and mistreatment, the message that abortion is a merciful deterrent to child abuse clearly involves a contradiction.

It has been suggested that the most effective way to combat the soaring divorce rate would be to do away with the institution of marriage, including all such existing unions. Can we also suppose that abolishing pregnancy might offer the best solution of all to the dilemma of abused children? Hardly. Yet, traces of this wayward thinking are contained in this section's introductory statement.

It is true that both a marriage and the onset of a child's life can be prevented. But we must not allow one sizable act to escape our notice — aborting a pregnancy in progress is not preventing abuse at all. For as divorce ''kills'' an existing marriage, so does abortion kill an existing child. There is a haunting illogic in seeking to curb child abuse by promoting the child's own death.

Abortion Forestalls Birth Defects

A number of years ago as I sat in my doctor's office awaiting an inoculation against rubella, a nurse told me, ''You're smart to have this vaccine now. You know, if you happen to be exposed to rubella while you're pregnant, we'd have to perform an abortion.'' This casual remark from a medical professional captures the predominant attitudes toward our handicapped sons, daughters, and patients in tidy summation. To the problem of fetal abnormalities, abortion has become a quick and easy — even expected — remedy.

With any pregnancy comes the risk of a defective child. However, certain circumstances such as a disease contracted by the mother, the chance that she is the carrier of a genetic disorder, her advanced age, or even a drug habit — to name a few — may indeed indicate a greater than normal cause for concern.

To approach a fair answer to the opening allegation, we must first recognize its triple impetus. And, while each of the three motivations is distinct in its reasoning, often it is some combination of them that compels the use of abortion for a defective or possibly defective child.

First, that a handicapped child will place extra burdens and demands on a family, both financially and emotionally, goes without saying. While raising any child these days is challenging, more work, worry, and, yes, perhaps even more tears may attend the rearing of an exceptional child. The added responsibility and financial drain may seem too much for a family to handle.

An extension of this concern stretches into sociological territory. Many would say that society shouldn't be obliged to ''bear the burden'' of these people either, that it is unnecessary to expend money and effort on their behalf and that such resources are better spent elsewhere.

In response to this first contention, I point out that the taking of a life to alleviate future economic and/or psychological stress for a family or a society raises an ethical imparity: a life for a nonlife. Life's value cannot be measured in terms of a person's future serviceability to the family or community into which he or she is born, nor by any financial encumbrances the individual may beget. Even in the shadow of such profound hardship, a human life is the ultimate wager. Surely an alternative other than abortion must prevail when the stakes are so high. Economics, family suffering, and individual duty must be renounced as concerns of a subordinate plane, for this issue is, peremptorily, one of life.

Designs for a superior race are positioned behind the second motivation for this argument. With eugenic fervor many insist that abortion is an effective and necessary avenue by which to filter the impurities of the human race, that the handicapped are useless and somehow don't belong with the rest of society, and, finally, that the whole is weakened by these "abnormal" parts.

But what constitutes "abnormal"? Someone missing a limb? Or one unable to see? As prenatal diagnosis and selective abortion become more widespread, where will this end? With stutterers? With left-handers? And who among us is fit to judge which persons are better plucked from the human mosaic?

In this high-handed purge, we could be rejecting some of our most valuable members. Those who are "special" are not to be sequestered and persecuted but, rather, cherished and loved in the company of the realization that there is no such thing as a "perfect" person and certainly not a perfect race. We are all members of one body, as Saint Paul says in his First Letter to the Corinthians: "Now you are Christ's body, and individually parts of it" (1 Corinthians 12:27). The body of Christ — all humanity — is compared to the human physique in that each member or part serves a different and unique function. Further, there are no lowly members, none less important than the others. Each, in his or her own way, is vital to the well-being and completeness of the whole. So, it might be said, that the closest point to perfection we, as a race, can possibly hope to achieve may come only through a fellowship of love, acceptance, and the joyful awareness that each one of us was created for a specific purpose commensurate with our abilities.

Are not we, as humans, infinitely inferior to our almighty Maker? Yet his eternal love and mercy are given freely and unconditionally to all.

It is not an uncommon belief that the degree to which a handicap hinders one's life is the amount by which the value of the life itself is reduced — that the "worth" of a person plummets with the severity of his other disability. Variations from a contrived image of "normal" are only those — variations not detractions. Many people who may be quite distanced from the "norm" lead rich and very satisfying lives — which lends focus to the third motivation.

This argument employs the assumption that anyone less than "perfect" cannot be truly happy and that elimination is the best possible answer for him or her. Many feel that a life laden with special hardships is not worth enduring.

But who is qualified to decide that for another? Which one of us has the right to choose death for someone as a reasonable alternative to living with any given malady? Can we be certain that death would be the choice of the person in question?

To justify killing an unborn baby "because he (she) wouldn't have been happy anyway" is a gross, shameful example of a logic that has jelled in the midst of the pro-abortion movement. If we endorse such an attitude, we are condoning murder as a logical solution to problems at any age (since conception to death is an unbroken chain of events) and for any lawfully approved reason.

Moreover, that it is possible to predict the future happiness or productivity of a person based upon his or her mental or physical capacities, or even family or social conditions, is an assumption that tramples not only all the precepts of common sense but the most vital lessons of Christianity and human good will. Let us not imagine, even for a fleeting moment, that the birth of any child might be a mistake uncaught by God.

Life, or the quality of being alive, is a gift that is precious in its own right. It may sometimes be agonizing or difficult or, at other times, quite enjoyable, but it is always a solely, self-executed endeavor toward personal contentment and fulfillment. It isn't feasible to forecast the happiness potential of any given person. Happiness is an individual experience and there is no universal criterion upon which to base its existence. In its truest, most enduring form, this emotion originates within a person. It is not shaped by external factors. In short, no one can instill happiness in another nor assess what happiness is for someone else.

C. Everett Koop, a renowned pediatric surgeon who has treated many deformed babies and children during his career, has expressed his observations of the handicapped in this way (as quoted by Bernard Nathanson): "It has been my constant experience that disability and unhappiness do not necessarily go together. Some of the most unhappy children whom I have known have all of their physical and mental faculties, and on the other hand some of the happiest youngsters have borne burdens which I myself would find very difficult to bear. . . . With our technology and creativity, we are merely at the beginning of what we can do educationally and in the field of leisure activities for such youngsters. And who knows what happiness is for another person?"[9]

As many who have worked with, lived with, treated, or taught them will attest, those who brook measures of incapability are often among the most motivated of people. There is no basis in truth for the notion that they enjoy life or life's experiences less than anyone else. The inner peace and self-acceptance that so many come to possess may be sorely lacking in "normal" people. (Could one reason be a blind, aimless struggle against not-so-patent handicaps — like selfishness, apathy, or arrogance?)[10]

Such are the motives behind the argument for abortion in the case of birth defects — the selfish, the eugenic, the presumptuous. However, abortions performed for this reason can be further categorized: those used to destroy babies with confirmed deformities and those done when there is only a suspicion or a chance of an abnormality. The use of abortion in this latter instance renders a disturbing conclusion: Everyday normal, healthy children are destroyed as "insurance" that a defective child won't "slip by" and be born.

For instance, as suggested in the opening paragraph, abortions are almost a matter of routine when a mother contracts rubella during the first trimester of pregnancy. Actually, according to R. E. Moloshok, the instance of birth defects in babies whose mothers had this disease is quite a bit lower than many might think — about 17%, and most are not terribly severe. What this indicates is that for each "abnormal" child aborted, five healthy ones are sentenced to be a medical "safety net" of sorts.

Following this twisted logic, why not allow all rubella babies to be born and then simply kill the affected one in six? This would allow life to the normal children and, after all, wasn't the original intention to be rid of the ''abnormal'' child anyway?[11]

Even staunch supporters of abortion might have trouble with this idea — a clear intimation of the ambiguous nature of their beliefs. There are some people who wouldn't dream of killing a ''born'' infant, but they might have considered abortion if they had suspected a deformity in the same child prior to birth.

However, much of the new thinking about unborn handicapped children is leaking into attitudes toward the ''just born'' handicapped as increasing numbers of these babies are intentionally starved and left to die in hospitals across the country.

To summarize, the impaired can be a blessing to their families and indeed to society. These ''special assignments'' can be lessons in patience, determination, and motivation. The love they can feel and that which they can inspire in others is unmatched in purity. They summon our power to serve without reward and demonstrate to us that real love is forged in the crucible of full acceptance. It was the finding of Rosalyn Darling, who has extensively researched attitudes toward the handicapped, that, with a sparsity of exceptions, children with some abnormality occupied a very special place in the family structure and in the hearts of its members. Further, although many expressed some degree of sorrow over having such a child, there wasn't a single case of parents who wished they didn't have the one they already had.

I cannot speak for the handicapped nor can I fully understand or appreciate their situations or special needs. What I do know is that I wouldn't want someone else to decide that ending my life was in my own best interest and for the good of all concerned.

How ironic that, in spite of recent measures to accommodate the impaired and to equalize or normalize their rights in society (access ramps, special restroom facilities in public buildings, parking privileges, closed-captioned programming, equitable hiring policies, etc.), they continue to be persecuted on this most fundamental level.

Truly, this brand of selective discrimination is alive and well.

All my being shall say,
   "O, LORD, who is like you,
The rescuer of the afflicted man from those too strong
      for him,
   of the afflicted and the needy from their despoilers?"
                                                    (Psalm 35:10)

Morality Can't Be Legislated

Throughout history some have questioned the right of the state to institute a moral doctrine. They have argued that the impersonal stipulations of law, in certain cases, amount to legislated morality — the antithesis of the belief that moral choices and decisions must originate in the hearts and consciences of individual citizens. Advocates of abortion have claimed that the right to an abortion is one such issue that is best removed from legal jurisdiction.

In pursuing the merit of such an assertion, we must first come to an understanding of the two primary types of morality. Individualistic morality, as its name suggests, concerns itself with the rights and interests of individuals. While the social form of morality acknowledges the rights of single persons, it is recognized that these privileges must fit into the context of a larger good — the good of the social order. And, in fact, ultimately the interests of the individual are best served in a selfless, altruistic environment.

It is in the spirit of this latter definition that all human societies have come to adopt certain universal moral standards as law. Foremost among these has been a traditional respect for life. This, and other subsidiary rights which may vary slightly from people to people and from era to era, has been recognized as self-evident when translated into secular law.

Although it is true that morality does indeed begin in the heart, it is equally certain that the survival of a harmonious society relies upon the existence of a framework of morally founded laws. If it

58

were permitted to each person to institute and live by his or her own codes of morality, collapse would befall society as we know it. In fast order, utter chaos would envelope a community of self-seeking individuals.

Imagine an intruder burglarizing your home. You call the police only to hear, "Sorry, we can't impose on him our belief that it is wrong to steal." So, the thief goes about his business, his personal "morality" unchallenged, and cleans out your house.

With abortion we are doing so much more than snatching household goods — we are stealing lives. And these tiny ones can't phone the police for help; they can't scream out in protest. They can't even try to change the law which allows their murders to be perfectly legal. They have no choice and no escape. Someone else's "rights" have left them the ultimate "helpless victims."

Those who feel with a de-legalized abortion policy they are being force-fed someone else's morality might do well to remember two points:

First, each day thousands of unborn children receive their parents' "morality" — in fatal doses — as abortion claims their lives.

Secondly, in some reasonable way, all law is "legislated morality," born of a need for an equitable system of justice and structured out of our interpretation of what is right and what is wrong, our perception of what is acceptable behavior and what is not.

Against everything from assault to petty theft to speeding on the roadways, laws are created to protect and preserve a fair, orderly, and safe community of citizens. A law forbidding abortion is nothing more than a natural extension of this legal intent. For our possessions, our homes, our rights, nay, our very lives are protected by this very same "imposed morality."

If we are honest with ourselves we know that, as individuals, all of our decisions, great and small, tap our pools of moral awareness. Trying to live and govern apart from the influence of morality is like trying to look at the night sky without seeing the stars.

Legalized Abortion Eliminates
Back-street Procedures

No one likes the idea of back-street abortions. The term conjures up frightening images of dark, musty rooms, or money-hungry abortionists and their crude, squalid instruments, of vulgar mistreatment and quantum risk. These conditions, according to pro-abortionists, fairly begged for legal reform. Why, when they would get an abortion one way or another anyway, subject women to such hazards of life and health? Why not legalize the procedure and provide a safer, cleaner way to abort?

Such vehement demands, framed by an overt sensationalism akin to what is often ascribed to the pro-life movement, were eventually instrumental in the abortion de-criminalization process.

However, during this crusade abortion proponents conveniently withheld mention of the fact that not all illegal abortions fit the "back-street" scenario depicted above. Before legalization, according to many sources, this type accounted for only about 10 to 15% of all illegal abortions. Of course precise percentages cannot be determined because of the veil of secrecy surrounding the underground abortion scene, but estimates have it that at least four out of five illegal procedures were done by qualified doctors — some of the same ones who perform them with the law's blessing today.[12]

So, the emotional ploys used were purposely misleading, and the exaggerated death rate from illegal abortions was a useful, if inaccurate, tool in eliminating the strict abortion laws.[13] We were led to believe thousands and thousands of young women were mangled beyond repair by underground abortionists and that death from infection and hemorrhage was common. Honest statistics assure us that the annual nationwide maternal death toll from illegal procedures was probably closer to one or two hundred — a slim fraction of one percent. Indeed, it is tragic that even one mother had to lose her life, but risks are inherent in any abortion, illegal or otherwise.

To grieve for all of abortion's victims seems natural — such needless loss of life! Somehow, though, the plight of the fallen children calls forth a distinct brand of mourning.

In view of the total picture, the incidence of maternal fatalities is overshadowed by the incredible number of baby deaths that abortion produces. Today, every sixty minutes or so, more babies face death through this legal channel of elimination than did mothers during an entire year of back-street procedures prior to 1973.

If this can be reduced to bare statistics, whom should the law have been protecting? A relative handful of women who knew the risks and yet had chosen to take the route they did or literally millions of innocent children who had no choice at all?

Protection of all of its citizens should remain the primary objective of the law. And a no-abortion policy is protection — for the children and for their mothers. Because, however surprising, many recent studies maintain that back-street or self-induced abortions continue today and have actually increased in some countries, even after the passage of quite liberal abortion laws.

Postulations for this rise include: an awareness that abortion is now readily available, resulting in more careless or accidental pregnancies; concern for secrecy; a panicked haste that wants to avoid the "red tape" of a legal abortion. Some may have allowed their pregnancies to progress to the stage where their own doctors no longer advise abortion. Often women, especially if very young and frightened, aren't aware of the legal channels and decide to accept the recommendation of a friend who "knows someone who can help." And, finally, many believe that since abortion is now legal, anyone who performs them is sanctioned by law.

It really matters not why some continue to participate in this pseudo-medical circus. The disturbing fact is, the legalities notwithstanding, they still do.

Even so, it's terribly wrong and logically unsound to legalize something because it can't be prevented. Should the use of cocaine be legalized? Or how about shoplifting or child abuse? There are many social problems which, at least in degree, are not containable by legal restraints. We don't respond by taking away the law.

Knowing that the law is at least a partially effective deterrent to crime, the logical conclusion is that a particular act would incur more offenders when legal than otherwise. Liberalization often begets abuse.

For instance, in the U.S. during the decade following the first year of legalization, annual legal abortions underwent an increase of 100% — from about 750,000 in 1973 to over 1.5 million in 1983!

These statistics evidence a progressive cycle — the more abortions that are performed, the more clinics and facilities that are organized to meet the high demand. As these clinics become a part of more and more communities, easier access to abortion sweeps across the land. Demand and availability feed upon each other.

Planned Parenthood, through its expansion and ongoing deployment of clinics, may be perpetuating the very conflagration it professes to want to control: unwanted pregnancies. (For more on Planned Parenthood, see Chapter Five.)

To review, the lawless carnage associated with back-street abortions is totally unacceptable. Concern for these women who are so frightened and desperate is shared by us all. But legalization wasn't the answer. Underground illegal procedures persist much like they did before 1973. Meanwhile the business of legal abortion, with its dreadful baggage of death, has boomed beyond all expectation.

Still, the crux of the debate lies not in whether or not legalization curtails grisly abortion practices, but rather in a searching appraisal of the procedure itself.

Abortion is a brutal, inhuman act yielding the same dire results regardless of the conditions under which it is performed. Varying circumstances do not alter the intent nor the outcome. So, the same reasoning that can attack other arguments for legal abortion remains applicable here despite the hollow contention that multitudes of women died at the hands of underground abortionists prior to 1973.

The summation of these sentiments compose the heart of the

matter and can be expressed quite succinctly: SANITIZING ABORTION DOES NOT ETHICIZE IT. For the child:

- Abortion is no less barbaric in an antiseptic hospital than in an alley.
- It is no less immoral under a white sheet than a gunny sack.
- It is no less painfully final with a curette than with a coat hanger.

Life Begins When *We* Say It Does

The small, two-man plane climbed to an altitude of 5,000 feet. When the aircraft leveled off and a cruising speed was established, the pilot opened his passenger's door and pushed him out of the plane to his death. On trial for murder sometime later, the pilot made a curious remark in his own defense: "It is true. I did push my passenger from the plane. But," he went on, "he would have died anyway had the plane crashed."

Of course this story is fictitious, but its logic is only too familiar. There are those, and they are legion, for whom abortion is acceptable until the child transcends that magic line of viability. The trust of their contention is that unless these little ones are able to sustain life on their own they needn't be protected or even acknowledged as anything more than a disposable mass of "tissue." As long as they couldn't exist in the outer world anyway, why shouldn't there be a plausible choice to abort?

This reasoning, in the light of serious thought, is exposed as utterly useless. For the point wrongly ignored is that the unborn child (a passenger of sorts in his or her mother's body) is not outside the womb nor is he or she likely to be until the natural, expected date of birth some weeks or months later.

Permission to abort an "inviable" baby and the testimony of the pilot are of a kindred logic. Both employ a strange line of inference to justify a harmful action. Both prey upon victims at a vulnerable point in time and space and then cite this vulnerability in self-vindication.

The forceful extraction of a child from the womb before birth, like the ejection of a man from the plane before touchdown, has little to do with life-sustaining abilities. Rather, they implicate only the most unscrupulous form of interference.[14]

Of no slight significance is the dispute over when abortion actually becomes a murderous act. The question of viability remains the epicenter of controversy. What does viable mean? What, if any, are the implications of its usage? And, finally, how befitting the unborn child is the term?

"Capable of living or maintaining life:" The dictionary defines viable in such a way that it is difficult to imagine a creature more viable — more resourceful in survivorship — than a developing infant. A brief review: from the depths of the child's own cells a blood supply is created as are the placenta, the umbilical cord, and, in fact, every part of his or her body and surrounding workmanship — each with a specific role to play in the life of the growing child, a design for the purpose of the little one's continued existence. Such an intricate wonder, this baby is splendidly and efficiently capable of living and maintaining life. This tiny being rises from a single cell and his or her command over the climate of the womb is, perhaps, the very pinnacle of viability.

The interpretation of viability preferred by pro-abortionists is tinctured with intimations of a support-free existence and of qualifying for legal validation. By this definition, viability has become almost synonymous with protectable life — but only in reference to the unborn. Once again a double standard is much in evidence.

Let us briefly consider an expanded application of this discussion. The same thinking that would excuse someone for killing an unborn child, because the little one is obviously incapable of "unassisted" life, would also be a legitimate defense in the case of a parent who left a small infant to die from neglect, or for someone who procured the death of a diabetic by withholding insulin, or for one who disconnected an iron lung, dialysis machine, or other life-support system. These theoretical victims, after all, occupy the same stratum of "viability" as the unborn baby — each merely relying on some outside device (and the unborn child only temporarily) to help sustain his or her existence.

At this juncture we should recognize the inherent and ongoing inviability in all humanness. Of course not everyone's "support" is as palpable as an iron lung for instance, but earthly sustenance is found in various forms — air, food, water, relationships with others. And while it is not my intent to split hairs, the foregone conclusion is that viability, in being a property that eludes a workable, communal definition, is an inept measure for the value and protectability of a life.

No sound distinction can be drawn between the various "supports" humans utilize during all stages of maturation and health. So, either all persons are viable or none are.

Moreover, we live in an age of intense medical advancement. The past two decades have brought crucial breakthroughs in the treatment of premature infants, effecting a significant drop in mortality rates. While a baby born in the seventh, sixth, or even fifth month of pregnancy may have had but a dismal chance of survival twenty-five years ago, the prognosis for the same baby today is much brighter thanks to these new developments. In fact, the smallest baby on record to have survived a premature birth reportedly weighed less than one pound.[15]

With each technological advancement the point of viability is swept a little closer to the very onset of life. It is not unreasonable to expect a future situation whereby fetuses can be "grown" and nurtured in laboratories. (Wouldn't it be a bizarre twist of fate if abortion is made obsolete not through human goodwill, but because a machine can execute maternal functions? Of course this propounds further ethical considerations and involves matters of overpopulation, infertility, birth control, even adoption and custodial rights which are outside the purposes of this writing.)

Viability, per se, is not a changing concept. Mortality rates aside, a baby at any given point of maturation has the same life and potential within himself or herself, whether born today or twenty-five years ago — and whether born in an upstanding American university hospital or in a hut in Botswana. The only element of change is the sophistication of the child's outside environment. Should the viability of a baby shift with the tides of medical efficacy? The diverse factors of time and global location notwith-standing, is it right to allow the baby's protectability status to be determined by the progress (or lack of progress) of the medical community into which he or she is born?

Let us not then ally ourselves with the opinion that human worth is buoyed by physical fitness or self-sufficiency. Nor let us allow that merited protection adhere to a timetable of trimesters. For protection and respect being "alive" should be qualification enough.

I offer the submission that "viability" as used in the abortion controversy is a slogan of convenience. Its open-ended definition only obscures the issue at hand. No logical, legal, or moral consistency is had in its unilateral application to the unborn.

Summary

The ad in the magazine read: "Solar-Powered Clothes Dryer. Will dry your laundry efficiently — uses no electricity! Price: only $60.00."

Many people, eager to curb their monthly utility bills, sent away for this revolutionary new appliance. What arrived in the mail several weeks later was nothing more than a retractable cord clothesline and a supply of clothespins — with a total retail value of about $12.00.

Needless to say, charges of fraud were brought against the company.

As the manufacturer knew, and as its patrons promptly dis-covered, language, carefully clothed, can be a tool of trickery and deceit. It can pervert truth and reality to fit intent. If one's intent is to swindle the unsuspecting consumer, as was the case of the clothesline manufacturer, an artful arrangement of words can be an effective sales ploy. By and large the American body of consumers is learning this and is becoming more prudent in its purchasing practices thanks to a growing awareness of consumer rights.

It is high time for a rousing awareness of perhaps the biggest fraud ever — the polemics of the pro-abortion cause. Its sugar-coated slogans have, in effect, "sold" abortion as a woman's right, a medical necessity, and a sociological good.

As we have seen, the abortion rhetoric can call abortion a woman's right while ignoring the rights of the child. Aren't equal rights for everyone?

The abortion rhetoric can label what's in the womb a "blob" or a "tissue," a "growth" or a "cluster of cells," when what is there must be a human life. Didn't everyone begin life as a tiny, arcane bit of humanity? And not a single such "mass of tissue" would develop into anything other than a fully fledged human person if not for natural or human-induced interference.

The abortion rhetoric can refer to the procedure itself as a "cleaning of the womb" or the "removal of conceptual tissues" when in reality invidious instruments or solutions are forced into the private world of the unborn to crush, tear, dismember, or burn.

The abortion rhetoric can entice us to believe that abortion is an "answer" to the problems of unwanted or deformed children, of pregnancy by force, child abuse, and overpopulation. Our good sense tells us killing isn't an appropriate response to any dilemma. In addition, according to C. Everett Koop, M.D., a full 97% of all abortions are performed for matters of economy and convenience. It's a smooth linguistic charm that can screen the hard fact of the matter which is: Each day thousands of children are pillaged of their lives because they represent an untimely burden to their families.

Human compassion and concern have become lost in a game of semantics — semantics that disguise the truth in a code of convenience; semantics that choreograph words around fundamental reality; semantics that continue to "sell" abortion to the uninformed "consumer."

Beneath this sugar-coated deception is a bitter pill to swallow. Abortion is murder. This doesn't change because we apply a new name. Remember, we can call our retractable clothesline a "solar-powered clothes dryer" or understand that it is a mere spiral of cord meant to be hung in the sun. We can call abortion a "procedure to empty the womb" or we can face the truth that it expedites the death of a fellow human being.

Deep inside a pregnant woman, the womb is astir with life. There is movement, growth, and the rhythm of a tiny heart. With a tremendous display of efficiency, the baby reaches new heights of maturation each hour.

After an abortion, the womb is empty and still. Where there once was a bustle of life activity, there is now a silent void. An ethereal world has been disrupted. A life has been dissolved.

Some question the nature of this life. Is it really human? Does it have rights? If the answer to the first question is "yes," and it is (what else could it be but human?), then the second question can have no other answer but "yes."

Life must be afforded preeminent priority. After all else it is the essence, the core, the polestar of the entire debate. It is where the abortion issue begins and where, too, it must end.

Since the dawn of legal abortion the unborn have been placed in a "no holds barred" competition with such rivals as convenience and economic and emotional comfort. What a wanton imbalance is perpetuated each time life is forced to vie with such lesser opponents. Yet this ill-fated battle has felled children in numbers beyond comprehension — nearly twenty million to date!

In summary, fallacy and beguiling misnomers are the spine of the abortion crusade. Truth is rejected, biological facts tossed to the wind. Both are quickly replaced with conscience-coddling phraseology like: "She opted to terminate her pregnancy, thinking it would be terribly unfair to bring a child into the world when she didn't feel ready or able to care for it." Under the cogent light of truth we come to see what really happens: "She paid her doctor to kill her child and remove him (her) from her body because she didn't want to be bothered with him (her)."

The pro-abortion movement is autism at work — in holocaustal measure. It is seeing what one wants to see, believing what one needs to believe to live by certain standards, all the while side-stepping objective truth. For even while all the facts militate to the contrary, the locution of its supporters continues to tout abortion as part of the "American Way."

Abortion on demand is not the badge of a free, democratic society. On the contrary, it is discrimination without compunction, domination without mercy. Wearing the guise of a civil right, it is oppression on a scale previously unknown to humankind. Its victims are the small, the voiceless, the powerless.

Call it what you will. Even murder can be made to sound sweet with enough pretty words heaped atop. And that, in simple, straightforward terms, is just what abortion is all about. Not pro-freedom, not pro-women, not pro-choice — but pro-killing. Abortion is, for any reason, excuse, or circumstance, human slaying human.

As Christians we must know that the license for the ending of a life belongs exclusively to the quintessential Giver of life himself.

Most assuredly and most unfortunately, there will always be those groping for "justifiable" reasons for killing the unborn. But there are none. So let them grope in their darkness. We can only pray that they see the Light. And, truly, it is easier to witness the Light after a journey through darkness.

CHAPTER FOUR

Effects of Abortion on the Mother

Unfortunate as they are, the maternal risks of abortion are of secondary importance to the purposes of this work. Its main concern remains the targeted victims. However, the dangers posed by legal abortion are an integral part of the process and, hence, merit note.

Abortion, like natural childbirth, is seldom fatal to the mother. According to author John Lippis, only thirty women of 100,000 will die as a direct result of a legal abortion (compared to fifteen during childbirth).[1]

However, abortion carries a profound rate of other maternal complications which often exceeds the danger of delivering a nine-month infant. Why are these risks so much greater in the aborted woman? After all, the baby and extra-embryonic matter are usually significantly smaller and seemingly "less trouble" than at full term.

Simply, because abortion is unnatural.

Physical Effects

In a woman about to give birth, the placenta is "ripe," the baby is ready, her muscles and hormones function in harmony with nature to relinquish the child to the outer world.

Abortion, on the other hand, is an unwelcome intrusion in a purposive biological process. It thwarts the efforts of a nature wildly devoted to nurturing the growing baby. The placenta and child must be prematurely "uprooted."

It is usually quite difficult to pick an unripened apple from a tree, while one that is "ready" will often drop at the slightest touch.

So it is with pregnancy — two bodies cling to one another, both instinctively abhorring the insurrection of abortion. Is it any wonder then that this violent overthrow might occasion adverse physical responses or reactions in the "host" life as well? The woman's body is robbed of a charge it intuitively and fervently protected. At the very least, abortion is an insult to her physiology.

Just what are the risks? And how frequently do they occur?[2]

Although many studies and reports continue to be published on this subject, statistics and percentages vary greatly from source to source.[3] While some may dauntingly sensationalize the effects of abortion on the woman's body, others understate the risks.

I shall try to discern a conservative average from the range of reports available, recognizing that exact figures shall never be known. The margin of variance is due to the large number of unreported abortions, the complications of abortions which are attributed to other causes, and even to the bias (pro-abortion or pro-life) on the part of those conducting the studies.

Nonetheless, to a woman who does suffer a negative physical reaction to abortion, whether through doctor error or as a result of the procedure itself, percentages mean nothing. If she is dying from hepatitis, there is no consolation in the fact that she had only one chance in 10,000 of contracting a fatal case of this disease.

Of course, many factors, including her condition, fetal size, and the method used, will play a part in determining the chance of short or long-term ill-effects for the aborted woman. The stakes are much higher in second and third trimester abortions, for instance, and for mothers in a generally poorer state of health.

Here is a list of the most common physical complications women must confront following an abortion and the percentage of women who suffer that complication. Some women suffer more than one such complication while others experience no physical complications.

Fever: 27%

Abdominal pain/dizziness/headaches: 25%

Infection: 25%

Menstrual irregularities: 12%

Significant hemorrhage: 5%

Need for transfusions: 2 to 5% (some reports go as high as 9%)

Laceration of the cervix (severe enough to require stitches): 4%

Readmission: 4%

Sterility: 4% to 25% (I strongly suspect 25% may be an ill-suited extrapolation, perhaps based on an isolated study, and that 4% more accurately represents the incidence of abortion-related sterility on the total population.)

Perforation of the uterus: 1.2%

Hepatitis: .5% or less

Death: .03%

Other risks include shock, blood clotting, nausea, abnormally rapid heartbeat, and, rarely, brain damage or salt poisoning (after a saline procedure).

Abortions may also influence subsequent pregnancies, effecting a three times greater chance of prematurity and an eight-fold increase in the risk of tubal pregnancies. Miscarriages are also twice as prevalent in women who have undergone abortions. Statistics for these problems indicate:

	Non-aborted women	Previously aborted women
Prematurity	5%	14-24%*
Tubal pregnancy	.5%	3.9%
Miscarriage	4.5%	14%
	*depending on number of abortions	

Emotional Effects

Women who seek abortions vary greatly, from the frightened young teenager to the sexually promiscuous woman for whom abortion is just another form of birth control and who may undergo several during her childbearing years. Reasons for wanting an abortion vary greatly, too, from "I'm too young" to "I'm too old" or from "I'm not married" to "We can't afford it."

To be expected, then, is a variegated spectrum of psychological responses in women following an abortion.

The reactions of friends and family members to her pregnancy and decision to abort and her experience with the staff of the clinic may also influence a woman's post-abortion state of mind. Was she put at ease and treated with respect? Or was she made to feel ashamed and "dirty"?

Whatever the circumstances, some type of emotional repercussions are unavoidable in the wake of an abortion. The only variable from woman to woman seems to be the degree of severity. While many are fortunate enough to escape major physical complications, a psychological price tag is always paid. A womb may be easily evacuated, but a mind is not.

Whether or not a woman believes she killed a "baby," she knows something has been destroyed — a part of herself? An inert fetus? Even the chance to have a baby? Of whatever opinion she happens to be, there is usually an accompanying feeling of separation or of loss. She faces a mixed package of relief and grief. Now rid of one unwanted predicament, she has taken on a whole new problem — and one that can't be "undone" or "aborted" — how to live in the aftermath of an interrupted pregnancy.[4]

For some this isn't so difficult, but for many others the abortion becomes an uncomfortable memory, a source of inner conflict that won't ever go away completely. A sense of sadness is common during the month in which the baby would have been born, and many have admitted that they pray for the child on each anniversary of the abortion. One girl said she broke into tears every time she saw a mother holding a new baby or pushing a child in a stroller. Another, incensed whenever a TV ad aired for baby food or disposable diapers, found herself constantly changing channels. Each woman deals with the loss in her own way.

Abortion flatly defiles the powerful, innate drive of a woman to safeguard and care for her young, and she often finds that whatever reason compelled her to make the choice to abort cannot quell the ache of this betrayed instinct. Post-abortion remorse may range from mild to intense, but, clearly, no woman can emerge from an abortion emotionally untouched.

Although there are percentages available on the emotional toll abortion takes, I fail to see how they can be anything more than loose estimates. Psychological changes induced by abortion are often far more subtle than are its influences on the physical being. How can the psychic upheaval of an abortion possibly be clinically evaluated and documented, especially when dealing with millions of women? And how can the effect of an abortion be distinguished from the effects of other incidents in a woman's life? We couldn't rightfully attribute every post-abortion suicide to the abortion! And perhaps there are longer-range emotional conflicts that haven't even begun to emerge. The human psyche is far too intricate for an accurate analysis in this area. It is for this reason I choose not to list percentages along with the following psychological "complications":

Depression
Guilt or a haunting conscience
Desire to be "punished"
Nervous disorders
Insomnia
Nightmares
Decreased work capacity
Decreased sexual libido
Frustrated motherhood or a petrifying of the maternal instinct
    (with older or subsequent children)
Regret
Psychosis
Suicide

The Dream

We lie upon the sun-warmed sand
My swollen belly and I
The ocean sounds so peaceful
Gulls play in the sky.

Then an icy wave breaks over me
I shudder beneath its bite
It washes away my pouch of life
And leaves me too numb to fight.

Tiny hands rise from the foam
Drifting farther out to sea
They grope and search but no one's there
I know they reach for me.

I awake with a flurry of heart
And a tense, beaded brow
The void is too much for me to bear
I wilt in pain, even now.

Outside, the squeals of children burn hot
Like an open wound on my soul
Pierced by their laughter, haunted by their joy
Am I obliged an endless toll?

Each time I see my baby's face
And hear his tiny voice
I know I shan't find the peace I sought
When I made that fateful choice.

CHAPTER FIVE

Harmful Influence of the Abortion Mentality

Let me take you someplace where children are taught
That murder is murder except when it's not.

That place is where the abortion ethic has moved in and taken over. Actually it is not so much a place as a condition of the social mind, an attitude, a mentality. It has "taken root," inculcating itself in the business of daily living. And dying.

For every three babies conceived in this country, one never reaches his or her "birthday" because of abortion. In some areas, abortions outnumber live births. Killing babies has become a fact of life.

The story comes to mind of a former co-worker as she recalled getting her first pair of prescription eyeglasses. Although just a young girl of about eight, her astonishment at seeing so clearly for the first time remained with her well into adulthood. She had believed the world was made up of the blurry images she'd always seen. For her, this fuzzy perception of her surroundings had been a fact of life. And, not knowing anything else, she thought everyone saw the way she did.

Many of the young people of today can't even remember a time when killing the unborn was forbidden by law. They have grown up in the midst of an ethical haze of sorts where the fact of abortion has risen to axiomatic status. The earth is round. The sun sets in the west. Free abortion is the law. How sad that for them "that's just the way it is."

As more and more children fall victim to this whirl of pestilence, it becomes increasingly difficult to turn our backs and say it doesn't affect those of us who don't participate directly. Because it does. Oh, how it does.

The mentality looms like a dark cloud over us all. With each day of death that passes we are learning to live in its shadow. In fact, abortion has become so fused into our societal landscape that its pollutant effects are inescapable. They are everywhere — sometimes where we least expect to see them. In a nation where abortion is commonplace, these insidious influences seep into the crevices of daily existence, touching everyone in one way or another.

All are in the grips of the mentality, not only the advocates of abortion but inactive pro-lifers as well who feel helpless to change it. With the draw of a vortex, the mentality sucks into its powerful current anything and anyone around it — forever changing not only a way of life but a way of looking at life.[1]

This section shall be dedicated to exploring the subtleties of the abortion mentality — the cultural backlash to legalization. They show up in the charities we support, the products we buy, and in the media. We shall think upon the equivocations that plague the priorities we set, the standards we live by, the legal system we employ, and even our world of medicine.

On Our Priorities

Recently, the local news ran a piece about a group of pelicans who were attacked and mutilated. Apparently an unknown culprit sawed off the top portions of their beaks, rendering the birds completely helpless and doomed to an "agonizing" death by starvation. The local stations were inundated with outpourings of public concern and financial support on behalf of the pelicans.

Not too long afterward, the story topping the newscasts was one of a whale lost in the river system north of the San Francisco Bay. Trapped in the shallow waters, it, too, was destined to die. Once again the viewing audience came to the rescue. Countless man-hours and hundreds of thousands of dollars later the wayward animal was guided safely back to the open sea.

Time and again we hear about the efforts of *Greenpeace* to save the whales or about people throwing themselves over baby seals to protect them from clubbers. There are groups dedicated to putting an end to the cruel, painful trapping of small animals for their furs.

Compassion for the earth's lesser creatures is one of the nobler of human instincts. It is natural and good to abhor cruelty to animals, to be repulsed by senseless slaughter or needless pain. And it is precisely this compassion that implores action to alleviate human suffering. Can we turn our backs on the needy members of our own species? Can we remain idle while abortion, for instance, claims victim after innocent victim?

Even before abortion became legal there were those who absolved themselves of all responsibility for their fellow human beings. Certainly abortion is not the cause of this disavowal, but the abortion mentality has magnified a distorted sense of priority and obligation. For example, during the ten minutes or so it took to air the pelican story, at least thirty unborn children succumbed to the curette or saline. They, too, were helpless victims. They, too, suffered an ''agonizing'' death, but quietly, secretly, and without any notoriety.

It is truly heart-wrenching to watch a baby seal being beaten to death while the mother seal looks on in horror. Even as this happens, though, dozens of babies undergo a brutal death of their own, with a saddened God as sole witness.

The distress of a child during an abortive procedure won't make the six o'clock news. The gruesome details of what happens to his or her body aren't headline material. Does this somehow assuage the emotional impact and lessen the importance of the ''cause''?

As Christians we shouldn't need an open or public display of tragedy to spur us to action, only a searching heart sensitive to even the unseen, unheard sufferings of our brothers and sisters. Something is terribly wrong when we demand the humane treatment of animals, when we bewail the unfeeling slaughter some of them must endure, and then sit by and do nothing to help unborn human babies on "death row."

Consider the significance of our Lord's earthly Incarnation. Did he assume the nature of a seal or whale? Did he walk the planet as a pelican or a monkey? Certainly not. God took on human form. He became one of us and in doing so conferred on humankind a crowning supremacy. He is intimately concerned, preoccupied if you will, with humankind in general and with you and me in particular. That this world belongs to the reign of humanity is a message beautifully conveyed in these words from Psalm 8:

> You have made him little less than the angels,
>   and crowned him with glory and honor.
> You have given him rule over the works of your hands,
>   putting all things under his feet:
> All sheep and oxen,
>   yes, and the beasts of the field,
> The birds of the air, the fishes of the sea,
>   and whatever swims the paths of the seas.
>
>   (Psalm 8:6-9)

Should not the energies of human compassion, then, remain within this most revered part of God's creation? Are we not called first to feed the hungry, clothe the naked, befriend the lonely, and free the persecuted among ourselves?

Let us continue to speak for the speechless, to rise in defense of the defenseless but always with the saliency of human need foremost in our hearts. We must be guided by conscience, not exposition.

Be appalled at the torment of animals.

But be appalled ten thousandfold at the destruction of human children. Let the sting of their deaths, the tragedy of futures lost, strike fear and empathy within the hearts of all. For however savage the treatment to seals, monkeys, rabbits, or minks, it can't quite compare to that which we inflict upon our own.

On Our Standards

If you've ever baked a cake or pie or made a casserole or soufflé, you might know that omitting even one ingredient will change the end result. Recipes are a carefully balanced blend of elements created to yield a completed dish that is just so.

The same might be said of the "recipe for humanity." Envision God as master Chef, skillfully intermingling people with unique personalities and talents, each with a measure of influence on the finished product.

Clearly then, the unharnessed use of abortion is disrupting the equilibrium of this and of future generations, not only in the much-publicized "Social Security scare" (the declining birth rate means fewer working citizens to support the "baby boomers" at retirement), but in a more abstract and perhaps more crucial capacity. It signifies an officious and irreversible intrusion into the natural tenor of humankind, indeed into the very course of history. In a very pragmatic sense, abortion has forever altered the character of the human aggregate.

The story that follows is thought-provoking yet certainly not unique.

About 200 years ago a woman sick with tuberculosis found herself expecting her fifth child. Her firstborn was blind, her second child had died. Her third was both deaf and mute and the fourth was also afflicted with tuberculosis.

Despite the "hopelessness" of her situation, this woman bore her fifth child, a son, and named him Ludwig van Beethoven.

True, the evolution of humanity without Beethoven may not have been tremendously different, but the void within the world of music would have been vast, although unbeknown to us.

The natural question is, who else is being shunted during the first lap of life? What other facets of our lives might be deprived because of the abortion epidemic? How has our world been affected without the presence and collective influence of our unborn, eliminated by abortion?

Are we losing friends, neighbors, spouses? Singers, dancers, performers? Architects, farmers, doctors, writers, teachers, scientists? And what about their contributions to society that we shall never know? A cure for disease, an answer to world hunger, a new invention? Why, the remains of the next Mother Teresa, Madame Curie, or Albert Einstein could be going up in flames (incineration is the number one method of disposal), even as you read this page. The point is we don't know and yet we continue to tamper with the natural direction of humankind and with the holy cadence of divine law.

The Christian recognizes every life as worthwhile and each person as having something to contribute to the world, whether here for two days or one hundred years, whether through music, politics, writing, or just the love he or she projects. Through a smile, a lesson, a word, an inspiration, each life touches the whole of humanity — each one of us is a piece of the puzzle which will reveal God's plan.

So the death of one can't help but affect everyone remaining, and in ways impossible to imagine. Even without regard to the idea of killing individuals, the thinking person is vividly aware of abortion's worldwide repercussions. Unless one is of the belief that human existence is purposeless and random, annihilation of such scope is understood to carry weighty effects which shall reverberate through all succeeding generations.

On Our Daily Life

One cannot live in this country during this era without playing some kind of role in the business of abortion. Yet our complicity in this wave of destruction may not be easily recognized.

On a public level, consider that our federal and state tax dollars fund a government that has legalized abortion. Whether or not we support abortion in theory, as tax-paying citizens we are forced to partake in this human demolition derby like helpless, nameless pawns. We are, in effect, supporting the lawmakers who initiated free abortion and the governmental structure which upholds it as law.

Thankfully, there are members of the political congregation who refuse to concede that the present law is the final word. Almost continually, new pro-life bills are introduced in Congress. However, we are not in a position to choose which side of this legal battle we can arm with our American dues. Therefore, our tax monies are often lost in the conflict while abortion on demand continues its reign.

Meanwhile, any government funding of abortion (i.e., medical programs for the poor, government-subsidized hospitals and clinics, insurance for government employees) contains traces of each taxpayer's dollar.

On a more personal level, what about our donations to charitable organizations and our dealings with abortion-related companies? It is in this area that we can exercise some control, exert some pressure to make our voices heard.

Donations to Charitable Organizations

Most of us feel a certain satisfaction with our *works of charity* — our charitable contributions to reputable groups and organizations. We are convinced that our donations will help someone, somewhere in need. What many don't realize, however, is that the abortion mentality is very insidious. It can enter in and begin to corrupt even the noblest of causes.

To cite an example, consider what has happened to The March of Dimes and its praiseworthy goal of eliminating birth defects. In recent years the organization has been promoting a technique called amniocentesis. This procedure involves the extraction of amniotic fluid through a hollow needle inserted into the mother's abdomen under local anesthesia. Bits of skin and cells shed by the child's body can be found in the withdrawn fluid. A culture is then grown for diagnostic study. Such an analysis can reveal much about the state and condition of the child, including incidence of severe abnormalities such as Down's syndrome, Tay-Sachs disease, spina bifida, and cystic fibrosis.

Amniocentesis can be applied with effectiveness during only a very limited time span, the earliest point of which is about sixteen weeks of gestation. Since the cultures need at least two weeks to grow, the pregnancy in question may advance to the fifth or sixth month before any diagnosis can be made.

The March of Dimes maintains it ''saves'' babies with the use of this technique and the related fetoscopy. That is certainly its stated intention. The organization claims that many women who are ''high risk'' (over 35 or with a family history of genetic disease, etc.) may be dissuaded from aborting after amniocentesis reveals no sign of fetal abnormality.

The other side of the coin discloses a less enchanting picture.

When the results of amniocentesis do identify a defective child, The March of Dimes offers counseling to the parents. Still, the majority of couples, 97%-98%, subsequently opt for therapeutic abortion. The removal of abnormal children is not a direct intent of The March of Dimes. In fact, the institution publishes some very sensitive and very optimistic literature about the special challenge of living with a handicapped child. But because of its program of widespread genetic screening, thousands of unborn children who fall short of the hopes and expectations of their parents lose their lives each year — probably many more than are ''saved.''

Ask yourself, should the unborn have to pass a genetic ''test'' before being allowed a live birth? Then ask some pointed questions of any group you plan to aid financially. The fight against birth defects is an important one. Would that it were carried on in the spirit of eliminating only birth defects, not those afflicted with them, and with the aim of saving all children while working to rid the world of these disorders altogether.

Dealings With Abortion-related Companies

Before considering the harmful effects of dealing with abortion-related companies, note the many types of "contraceptives" on the market.[2] They "prevent" pregnancy by functioning in three distinct ways. 1) They can thicken the mucous plug at the cervix, preventing the sperm from entering. This is truly a contraceptive effect. 2) They can prevent release of the ovum, temporarily sterilizing the woman. This is also clearly contraceptive. 3) By hardening the uterine lining they can preclude the implantation of the week-old human cluster of cells. This tiny being is then passed from the mother's body without notice. This is not contraception but abortion.

What is the status of the various pills on the market? The earlier, high-estrogen pills largely prevented ovulation (#2 above). Many of the newer, low-estrogen pills also attempt to interfere with ovulation (#2) but have a higher "failure" rate so they include an anti-nidatory effect (they harden the lining of the uterus, #3 above). According to Dr. J. C. Willke, the "morning after pill" sometimes acts in a sterilizing fashion (#2), depending on when ovulation occurred, and sometimes acts as an abortifacient (#3). As far as the intrauterine device (I.U.D.) is concerned, with a few exceptions, almost all scientific papers agree that it acts abortively (#3). Many women who employ these methods of "birth control" are aware of their interceptive technique. However, I suspect that there are some women (and husbands and boyfriends, too) who might be troubled knowing they had initiated a number of "secret," ill-fated pregnancies.

Again, the key is to be informed.

Upjohn, a major drug company, markets prostaglandin which is used in abortions. The hormone induces premature labor during any stage of pregnancy. This company also manufactures scores of other medications and pharmaceuticals which fill the shelves of drugstores nationwide. When we buy any one of its products, whether it be cough syrup or bicarbonate, we are patronizing a company with anti-life policies.[3]

Increasingly, advertisements for collagen-enriched makeups, hand creams, and shampoos beckon us from our television screens and from the pages of many periodicals. Considering the times we are living in, it's not surprising that some people have wondered whether this special protein might have been derived from fetal material. Naturally, reputable cosmetic companies are anxious to dispel this rumor. They insist that the collagen in their products is either of animal origin or, occasionally, derived from human afterbirth (the placenta and other membranes expelled after the birth).

With regard to this last point, Dr. Willke remarks: "After the child is born, he or she no longer needs the placenta. For many years, hospitals have frozen and sold them to drug companies to extract hormones and other substances. More recently, placentas have been sold to cosmetic manufacturing companies. This may be distasteful or even revolting to many people. There is, however, no major ethical problem in such use."[4]

But there is a related ethical problem looming on the horizon that makes the collagen question seem almost insignificant. If the promise of a wrinkle-free complexion is enough to suggest the commercial use of fetal tissue, what if this highly adaptable tissue were touted as actually being able to cure a whole spectrum of *major illnesses?* Imagine the pressure that would be applied to medical researchers to quickly verify this. "Certainly," the argument would go, "minor ethical questions should be brushed aside if the possibility exists that the use of these readily available fetal tissues will mean so much good achieved, so many lives bettered, and so much human suffering alleviated."

That time has already arrived. Writing in the *National Right To Life News,* editors Dave Andrusco and Leslie Bond state: "Although there is some controversy, reporters say, transplant surgeons are developing a 'miracle cure' for everything from slight hearing loss to Parkinson's disease. The source of this cure-all, described as a veritable 'fountain of youth,' is tissue taken from the bodies of aborted babies.

"Researcher after researcher, hospital after hospital, medical school after medical school is jumping on the bandwagon. There are perfunctory remarks about 'ethical issues raised' and the like but there is an aura of inevitability to their comments. And why not, if as one exuberant proponent put it, fetal tissue techniques are 'to medicine what superconductivity is to physics'?"[5]

Andrusko and Bond detail several aspects of the controversy and then add: "But all these reasons are amplifications of the core objection: that the source for these transplants is aborted babies unjustly killed by a society which has no use for them alive but which cannot wait to feast on their remains. . . . As others associated with the transplants have quickly learned, it is virtually impossible to separate the 'miracle' tissues — said to possess the key to curing Alzheimer's disease, leukemia, sickle-cell anemia and epilepsy, to name just a few of the applications — from their source."

Proponents argue that these tiny babies "are going to die anyway." Pro-life people counter with, "That argument was used at Nuremberg as a defense for the atrocities committed by doctors in the Nazi death camps. It was rightly rejected then, as it must be now."

Other critics, such as Jeremy Rifkin, cite still other reasons to oppose the use of fetal tissues. His major objections are twofold: First, he alleges that some physicians do not perform proper determination of death on aborted infants before removing their tissues — leaving open the possibility that at least some of these babies are being harvested alive. Second, he claims that the sale of fetal tissues or organs should be strictly prohibited under the Organ Transplant Act of 1984, which bans the sale of human body parts.

Andrusko and Bond point out that since 1985 "the field of fetal tissue transplants has virtually exploded, prompting one proponent to claim 'a new age of science' and one journalist to predict 'a new form of surrogate motherhood, in which women get pregnant for the purpose of getting abortions and selling the victim's remains.' " They conclude their article with this statement: "According to Rifkin, we as a society are now at a crossroads, and the choices are clear: We can continue along the path of a utilitarian ethic, in which all things — including life itself — are reduced to mere 'commodities'; or we can 'resacralize' life and return to a world in which life is treasured and respected.''

Surely, the sordid business of abortion is everywhere. It has seeped into the mainstream of American life, forcing everyone — regardless of personal conviction — to be a participant in one way or another. If that isn't bad enough, we are thrown so many covert obstacles that we must continually be on guard to avoid them. Charities and manufacturers that have their hands in the abortion industry don't readily advertise such involvement. Meanwhile whole segments of the medical profession are betraying their own traditional ethics by embracing the false principle that ''the end justifies the means,'' even though the ''means'' of choice is the wholesale slaughter of innocents.

So we must make it our business to be aware! The opportunities to choose life are everywhere. Good intentions are simply not enough. We have a responsibility to ourselves and especially to the unborn to be informed and to renounce all involvement, directly and indirectly, with the practice of abortion.

On Our Respect for Life

While window shopping, an elderly gentleman happened into a quaint, little antique shop. He immediately noticed three showcases, each filled with assorted vases, porcelain figurines, paintings, and other art objects.

On the first showcase hung this sign: ''All items $25.00.''

On the second the sign read: ''All items $100.00.''

And on the third: ''All items $500.00.''

The gentleman noticed a striking similarity in the contents of the three cases and, in fact, after close scrutiny could detect no apparent distinction in the quality of the pieces.

He directed his bewilderment to the shop's owner, a tiny, gray-haired man with an unmistakable twinkle in his eye. The owner sat in thought while he carefully lit his pipe. Smoke curled around his head as he spoke. ''Human nature is a funny thing.

People believe what they choose to believe. If someone comes in here wanting a small, inexpensive vase for a bedroom bureau, he naturally will select an item from the first showcase. On the other hand," he went on, "if a collector desires a piece for display, he might shop the third showcase." He paused as if wondering whether or not to continue. "I'll let you in on a little secret," he said. "Each piece in the three cases shares a common market value, yet I sell about the same number of items from each of the three groups."

He grinned at the shopper's obvious astonishment, and then added: "Please don't tell anyone. It might be bad for business."

"But isn't this illegal?" queried the window shopper.

"I let my customers place their own 'value' on the items," replied the owner. "They pay what the piece is worth to them. I assure you I am cheating no one."

"How much are these really worth?" asked the shopper.

The owner's eyes twinkled. "You believe as you see fit."

As the mystified shopper was leaving the store, he noticed a photograph of what must have been the owner's grandchildren sitting atop his desk. He smiled to himself as he read the hand-written caption: "Priceless."

What determines something's value? What criterion measures worth? People assign value to "things" all the time. Retailers impart a value to articles of clothing, food items, furniture, jewelry, even units of electricity. Services are also sold at a price, like how much you must pay someone to fix your TV, take away your garbage, or cut your hair. All in all, such estimates of worth — "thing value" — are relative. They fluctuate with supply and demand, individual needs and wants, trends and fads, and with the state of the economy. They are not absolutes.

If you were to ask a man on the street what he considered to be more valuable, diamonds or water, chances are he would answer "diamonds." And, in a way, he would be right. In our country water costs less than a penny a gallon while a diamond may be worth hundreds, even thousands of dollars, depending on the size and quality.

But, ask the same question of someone lost in a sweltering desert and you will likely get a completely different response. Water, in this case, might be worth more than a truckload of the finest diamonds. "Thing value" is heavily circumstantial.[6]

At a point outside the peripheries of monetary value or sentimental value or any other value that originates within human society or is placed by society is intrinsic value. Such worth is fixed in the very nature of an entity. It is valuable because of what it is, not because an oil tycoon or an art critic deemed it so.

Here, then is laid an important distinction — one to be kept in mind as we embark on a discussion of human worth.

Who would dispute that a person carries an infinite, intrinsic worth, immeasurable by a fluctuating earthly criterion? People are valuable not because of their function in society or because they happen to align with the wishes and needs of others. No, human beings are valuable because they are precisely that, a part of humanity, and because the Investor of human worth, God, is infinite and unchanging.

Christ Jesus died to redeem us, one and all, in an act that would become the ultimate testimonial to our sovereign standing on the divine hierarchy. His blood is humanity's salvation and it is this blood, finally, that ordains worth. Lest we think that this worth must be earned or accrued, consider how the Lord gained admittance to our world. That he himself, on a par with his earthly brothers and sisters, underwent all phases of human biological development both in and out of the womb is a fact which should, once and for all, explode the mind-set that human worth somehow comes into existence at birth and not before. As a human being can't be "partially" alive (he or she is either alive or not), neither can his or her worth be partial. Even as the person is being created, at the very moment a new child of God is coming into being, his or her worth is already whole and indissoluble.

So, people have value precisely because they are human beings — which is what God chose to become. Thus, the sacredness of human life is an absolute and respect for this gift of life is not a choice, but a grand obligation.

To stray from this is the essence of sin. All violence and prejudice has at its heart a perverted image of human worth — a due veneration supplanted by the likes of greed, arrogance, or apathy. It begins with a redefinition of personhood, a reassessment of the respect that was once the acknowledged right of every human being.

From a sociological purview, history has witnessed the tragic consequences that ensue when a certain group or race is excluded from the sphere of valuable and protectable personhood.

During much of the eighteenth and nineteenth centuries, Blacks were disavowed.

During this century, another bitter lesson was written when the Third Reich dehumanized millions of Jews during the Holocaust. Although it is not my intent to allege a moral correspondence between the Nazis of the 30s and 40s and the pro-abortionists of today, the motivation behind the horrors of the concentration camps and of Black thralldom can be likened to the impetus behind the horrors in today's abortion chambers. At the core of this unhallowed behavior is a change of attitude — a reevalution of personhood and human worth. No longer is a person valuable simply because he or she is, but only if and when that person meets contemporary standards of acceptability.

In an earlier chapter I wrote of autism, the inclination to look at life in terms of one's own needs and desires, heedless of objective truth. Nowhere in recent history was reality so pliant as in the minds of the murderous Nazis and the White slave owners of yesteryear — unless it is in the hearts of today's abortion advocates. If this brand of sociological categorization fueled the historical persecution of Blacks and Jews, it is positively thriving in the abortion mentality of today. People find it convenient or socially advantageous to think of certain groups of people (namely, the unborn) as ''non-persons'' and to deal with them on a subhuman level.[7]

By mocking the absolute merit of each person, the abortion mentality has propelled us into an age where lives are measured and human value is well-nigh as relative to circumstance as ''thing value." The implications are frightening and the questions raised not easily answered: Are some unborn children worth more dead than alive? Who decides when life and death interference is "legitimate"? How can ending one person's life be less evil than ending another's?

The abortion ethic, in failing to reconcile these burning questions, transfers God-authority to anyone who can conceive. And this is humankind's ultimate threat — not guns or knives, not pollutants or chemicals, not even nuclear arsenals. The most virulent weapon, which humanity has turned upon itself, is its assumption of jurisdiction in this area of placing value on its own members.

Embracing abortion as a social requisite had a devastating effect upon our sense of responsibility to our fellow human beings. Once respect for one form of life is lost and the safeguards protecting it surrendered, reverence for all life is reduced to some degree.

What, we might ask, is next on this deadly list? Who will be the victims of the next wave of a fastidious society? Many believe infanticide is the next natural stepping-stone along this lethal continuum. Pro-lifers are often accused of conjuring up ugly stories of newly born babies being killed for the same reasons abortions are allowed.

But such is not wild prognostication rooted in paranoia. The "unthinkable" is already happening.

One case in point is the story of an infant boy born with Down's syndrome in April of 1982 in Indiana. By a decision of his parents which was upheld by the Indiana Supreme Court, the child was denied food, water, and medical aid. This death sentence was carried out despite numerous couples offering to adopt the child. He died at the age of six days.[8]

Some may say it's for the best, for the mother could have aborted months earlier anyway had she known the condition of her child. The end result is the same, right?

Such a liquid sense of obligation has no mooring! Will we next be entitled to kill our children because if we'd known they'd keep us up all night or wet the bed or flunk math in school we'd have chosen not to bring them into the world in the first place?

And then who? The elderly? The poor? The useless? As we hear of more and more "Baby Does" dying needlessly in hospitals and of other "mercy killings," it becomes painfully apparent that our society is at a point of low resistance to the further transgressions of a waning respect for life. Consciences are dull, priorities turbid.

Certainly, the burden of every "wrongful" death cannot be placed on the shoulders of free abortion, but rather on the same social precept from which abortion itself was born. However, the uncontained use of intrauterine murder has made it progressively easier to accept other forms of social killing. Not only have reports of infanticide and euthanasia increased at alarming rates since legalization, suggesting a moral cousinage, but we approach previously untraversed depths with such practices as sex-screening of the unborn. (After testing determines the gender of the child, the parents may opt for abortion and the chance to "try again" for a child of their preferred sex.)[9]

Abortion on demand is a breach of Christian law and a definite threat to a civilized society because it promotes death as a solution to personal and social problems.

As we struggle with the increasingly cloudy boundary between "good killing" and "bad killing," we face a future of grave uncertainty. We are letting life itself slip through our fingers and the light of the world grows a bit dimmer with each such failure of heart. Without a rebirth of commitment, without an uncompromising fidelity to the homage and respect due all forms of human life, I fear the world's light, the world's hope, will steadily and irreparably disappear.

On Our Human Sexuality

Sexuality is, as is no other aspect of humanness, a fire of body and spirit. A confluence of individual disposition, moral fortitude, and raw instinct, it is a force that drives its roots into the deepest self. One's use (or misuse) of his or her sexuality is perhaps the most telling measure of self-image and self-worth.

Since abortion and sexuality are intractably linked in that the former would be completely unnecessary without the passions of the sex drive, to what extent might the abortion mentality influence the individual's view of his or her own sexuality?

To answer this we need to study society's collective reaction to abortion, since one's attitude about sexuality is at once intensely personal and hopelessly reliant upon environment.

In retrospect we can observe a declining strength in the fundamental family structure and the traditional code of values. The past years have been prodigal of "illegitimate" pregnancies, venereal disease, "open" marriages, skyrocketing rates of divorce, gay-rights movements, surrogate motherhood, and rife pornography. Some call it a state of moral breakdown — others label it a time of long-overdue sexual liberation. Whatever the case may be, many situations and philosophies which once drew social opprobrium are now condoned, even encouraged. Public stigmas no longer exist in any imposing or constraining form.

Certainly this cultural shift cannot be attributed to the practice of abortion. It was beginning long before 1973 brought legalization. But the fact that "free" love and promiscuity reached new heights during the same decade that we saw the first stirrings of the abortion movement indicates a correlation of some latitude.

Just what is that correlation? How has abortion flavored the contemporary ethos?

Very simply, abortion fosters a decaying sense of sexual worth by scorning the eternal goal of human sexuality.

As presented in scriptural theology, sexuality is a divinely endowed gift, bestowed upon humankind by a truly loving God. As we blossom into full, physical maturity we accrue an awesome responsibility and privilege. With the burgeoning power of creation within us we stand in the company of life's Author. But more than just an agent for continuing the race, sex is meant to be an integrating factor of caring relationships — a thread which strengthens the very fabric of love. God's ordained design for sex is graciously twofold, allowing for both the procreation of children and for the expression of deep, committed love.

The oneness of sexual union, in its purest and most perfect sense, has been loftily equated to the union between Christ and his Church. If we can fathom the full significance of this gift and the breadth of the love with which it is given, then abortion can only be seen as a blight which strips human sexuality of all dignity. For when sex is practiced freely outside the framework of marriage (not to mention love), and its fruits are destroyed almost as freely, what we have in our midst is but a travesty of what good, salutary sexuality is all about. The sacred function is perverted beyond any hint of God's purport.

Abortion hasn't caused this headlong dash into the sexual revolution, but its widespread use has been a factor of no minor significance in its duration and level of intensity.

First, it offers a quick "solution" to one of the "undesirable" side effects of free love, confusing the basal instincts and fomenting an irresponsible attitude toward sex. Even more, abortion is a hostile invasion of the most delicate province of human sexuality — an invasion which derides God's Word and violates the divine purpose of the sex act itself.

When sight of the quintessential meaning of sexuality is lost on the larger social scale, it becomes increasingly difficult for individuals to retain a sense of their own sexual importance and worth. Even for those whom abortion hasn't touched directly, just knowing it is there, for the asking, makes a mockery of sexual value. Without this appreciation of self-value, there is every danger of exploiting the powers of sexuality — of glorifying pleasure and permissiveness. The terminus of a sexual encounter becomes not a welcome for a child nor a mature closeness with another, but an outlet for self-gratification.

This is not to say one must become a parent to realize a sexual completeness. No. It is only to observe how easily this tool of love and reproduction is misused — and at what price? The energetic pursuit of abortion, to the disregard of our spiritual, emotional, and physical selves, is a costly discipleship indeed. It shatters the composite of the whole sexual person. And this, then, is the full recompense — a twisted, misdefined sexual purpose. Truly we have arrived at the nadir of moral descent when carnal pleasure has become the ultimate deity and when children in the womb are referred to as "a sexually transmitted disease."

The abortion mentality has breathed a vile, unnatural air into the dynamics of human sexuality. No wonder so many seeking fulfillment in the new liberation find only confusion and dissatisfaction. It is a liberation, abetted in part by abortion, that has abandoned the profound meaning of individual sexual worth.

On Our Common Sense

Behind the "liberal" facade of the pro-abortion cause is a mindset teeming with contradictions and streaked with paradox. A blatant rejection of the time-honored tenets of a civilized Christian society, the abortion mentality is a veritable morass of logical and moral ineptitude. It just doesn't make sense.

A most noteworthy example of this assault on our common sense is found in the medical community whose acceptance of abortion marks a strange evasion of a long-known scientific fact — that human life begins at conception. Try and digest this highly confused situation:

Fact: A six-month "preemie" lying in an incubator cannot be killed and in fact enjoys all of the latest tools of medical technology employed for the preservation of his or her life.
Fact: A six-month womb-bound baby can be killed.

Fact: For a happily pregnant woman who goes into premature labor, a doctor will try to postpone the delivery of her child until the little one reaches a more optimum point of development.
Fact: The same doctor may induce early labor on a not-so-happily pregnant woman.

Fact: A child in utero who is killed through an accident is generally regarded as a person. How many times have you heard something like this on the news: "The death toll from that accident has been officially increased from 23 to 24. One of the women was found to have been pregnant."

Fact: A child destroyed by abortion is not even acknowledged as such — just as fetal tissue, product of conception, uterine contents, etc.

Fact: The smallest baby on record to have survived a second-trimester birth reportedly weighed a scant 12 ounces.

Fact: Many aborted children weigh anywhere from one to four pounds. (Occasionally even more.)

Fact: Surgery cannot be performed on a minor without parental consent. In an emergency situation, medical personnel will frantically search out the parents or guardians for permission to operate or perform the necessary procedures.

Fact: In many states, minor girls can undergo an abortion without parental knowledge or approval.

Fact: By a statement of the American Medical Association which contends they are healers whose job it is to cure not kill, physicians are not allowed, despite personal convictions, to administer a deadly injection in an execution.

Fact: Physicians may inject a lethal saline solution into the amniotic sac containing a growing child.

Fact: Many still contend that the unborn child is but a "potential" human being and is not yet "alive."

Fact: Much to the dismay of hospital personnel, abortions sometimes "fail" resulting in the births of children who are very much alive. (If they die, however, on their own or with a little "help," the doctor must complete a certificate of death.) An adjunct to this contemplation: Not too long ago a bill was introduced in a state legislature regarding a policy of anesthetizing babies before the abortion procedure is begun. (Why anesthetize a "lifeless blob"?)

Fact: If a patient dies under incompetent doctor care a "wrongful death" suit might be filed.
Fact: "Wrongful birth" suits (a term minted by the abortion mentality) have been initiated by parents after their babies were born with defects that could have been detected during pregnancy.

Fact: Some physicians in abortion hospitals refuse to do late procedures, finding it difficult to grapple head on with the sheer evidence of life.
Fact: These physicians will kill a child in an earlier, less "vivid" stage of development.

Fact: On the other hand, there are doctors who will only perform saline abortions, knowing the injection marks the end of their involvement. They need never see the delivery of the dead infant.
Fact: For many of these doctors watching tiny baby parts as they are drawn through the tube or scraped from the womb is too unpleasant.

To recap, in order for the medical society to accept a child as a person and to acknowledge and uphold his or her right to life, any one of the following conditions must first exist: Either, 1) the child must be outside of the mother's body, or 2) the child must be wanted by the mother, or, ironically, 3) the child must be fatally injured through some type of accident. God help the child if the answer is "none of the above."

Another example of this assault on our common sense is evident when we examine the medical grounds for "proof of life." Here we are offered another taste of the self-serving thinking that is so much a part of the abortion mentality.

In this day of advanced technology when machines can almost "live" for a person, the distinction between life and death is not always readily apparent. With the nearly unlimited ability to sustain physical existence comes the grave responsibility of management in an area that involves so much more than the disciplines of medical science. Here we are enjoined to weigh moral, theological, and volitional considerations as well.

The profession that deals so intimately with life and death has borne the brunt of this responsibility. Daily, physicians and the families of the critically ill or injured must make choices that somehow seem to eclipse even the best of human judgments, yet which have been forced upon us by technological progress. It is a fine line to walk when often the only link with life is a thread of electricity.

This is not meant to be a discussion of euthanasia. Rather it is to point out that perhaps at no time in history has it been more crucial to establish a concerted, workable definition of life.

By and large a patient is considered to be alive as long as his or her heart and brain are operant, no matter how hopeless or irreversible the physical condition. It is only when these organs cease to function that a doctor will pronounce death. The use of life-support is countermanded only after more than one E.E.G. (electroencephalogram) reveals brain death.

In the womb a child's heart begins beating three weeks after conception (usually before confirmation of pregnancy) and his or her brain shows measurable activity about three weeks after that. ("Measurable" means able to be detected by currently used equipment.) When abortion is the accepted policy, the child's *life* is not acknowledged at all. The very characteristics essential to satisfy our definition of life become absolutely meaningless.

Have a number of our doctors, who are members of the profession that pledges its very being to the service of humanity, actually espoused a mind-set that's so blatantly contemptuous of human life in the womb?

Sadly, some have. Incredibly, they've managed to separate the idea of *abortion* from the idea of *killing*. This schizoid pattern of thinking has allowed them to assume the double role of both healer and killer. Such a dualistic approach to medicine should not be tolerated.[10]

Lest this appears to be an attack on all doctors, I must point out that the practices of most specialized physicians (neurosurgeons, optometrists, dermatologists, orthopedists, to name a few) have little connection with the science of embryology or the use of abortion. I also must mention, with great admiration, those general practitioners, gynecologists, and obstetricians who will not make referrals for abortions, sometimes risking persecution, ridicule, and the loss of future referrals themselves because of this position.

Pro-life medical students, too, may find themselves in a difficult situation. Often they must witness an abortion as a requirement of a course. Many hazard failing, not to mention the scorn of their fellow classmates, in their decision not to take part.

Clearly, organized medicine, in its wedding with abortion, has struck a posture that is utterly incompatible with the biological facts. This precarious disposition betokens an extreme change in the policy of a historically altruistic science.[11]

In today's world, the annihilation of tiny humans is a "medical service," right up there with the removal of tumors, appendixes, tonsils, and warts. Indeed, abortion has added a new dimension to the services of modern medicine.

On Our Legal System

"The care of human life and happiness and not their destruction is the first and only legitimate object of good government."
— Thomas Jefferson, 1809

By now it is commonly known that our government allows and even supports the burning, poisoning, and dismembering of unborn children through abortion, yet provides stiff penalties for anyone who would inflict these same tortures on a child outside of his or her mother's body. But, did you know that there are cases where the legalities are even more obscure and where the child's presence in the womb doesn't necessarily guarantee absolution for anyone who would kill him or her, intentionally or otherwise?

Recently, the local news presented an example of this penal double standard. It seems a man was involved in an automobile accident which resulted in the deaths of unborn twins. He was charged with second degree murder! To convict this fellow, malicious intent would have to be proved.

How odd, I thought. Had the babies been aborted, who would have questioned the attending physician — let alone indicted him for murder? And it would be difficult to imagine a situation involving more "malicious intent" than an abortion. It is a deliberate, premeditated destruction of a human life — and isn't that the very definition of "murder"?

Also in the news is a woman on trial for continuing to use narcotics during pregnancy despite the warnings of her doctor. The son born to her was brain-damaged and lived only five weeks. To think she might be penalized for the consequences of her drug abuse when a doctor could have accomplished the same end, directly and legally!

At this discussion of penalties I am reminded of a passage in Bernard Nathanson's book, *Aborting America*. Dr. Nathanson, himself a former abortionist, expresses this opinion regarding abortion and punishment: "The penalty for abortion, in my view, must be less than that for homicide, but neither should it be handled like a traffic ticket."[12]

Are we to pass sentence on the basis of the victim's size or age? If so, surely it is a more horrible crime to take the life of a six-foot individual over one who stands only four foot eight inches. And how much worse the offense to murder a senior citizen than, say, a teenager!

Or, perhaps we are to prescribe punishment in proportion to the grief brought about by death? If such is the case, the more friends and relatives a victim leaves behind, the stiffer the penalty would be for his or her murder.

I call attention to this not to disparage Dr. Nathanson who has done much to further the pro-life cause, but only to elucidate a strange twist in the law. Because the unborn aren't really "known" or "established" in a family or society and their deaths might not carry the same impact as a born individual, are we to mitigate the penalty for murder?

Any way you look at it, abortion is homicide. Pure and simple. It is the planned, intentional killing of one human being by another. Until it is accepted as such, the legal regime which permits it shall remain inherently at variance with the truth.

Another consideration: with one hand, our government grants money to hospitals and clinics for the task of killing unborn children, with the other it doles out funds to their *in utero* counterparts who were declared citizens and found eligible to receive Social Security benefits, estate settlements, and welfare payments.

Parental rejection divests the unborn child of all the natural rights of citizenship, including basic protection. Apparently, the onset of American citizenship is a fluid point, relying on the circumstances and attitudes involved.

Yet another conundrum is the status of fatherhood. With their rights finally being recognized and acknowledged, fathers are enjoying an overdue expansion of legal and social privileges. Today we see them involved in prenatal classes and many are present during the deliveries of their children. More and more fathers are happily accepting an active part in the rearing of their children with a surprising number taking over the role of primary caretaker which traditionally belonged to the mother. Especially noteworthy is the increased number of fathers who win custody of their children after a divorce — and even in some cases when no marriage took place at all.

Indeed, their rights as parents are finally commensurate with the ligature of mutual need between father and child and with their function as equal biological contributors to new life — with one burning exception. If the mother decides to kill his unborn son or daughter, the law gives a father no rights whatsoever. He is as helpless and as victimized as his baby.

And the same legal system that won't acknowledge his rights

before birth, in a show of utter polarity, will demand his parental duties in the form of financial support after his child is born.

Distorted priorities are evidenced once again as we realize that in this arena of paternal rights, a child's source of income is a more prudent concern than his or her very life.

The list of these legal lunacies goes on, but the point is well made. In a civilized nation where human life has peak value, to espouse the blatantly self-contradictory policy of destroying life in the name of convenience or social good is bound to create gaping "holes" and inconsistencies in the legal weave.

However vigorously we seek the separation of Church and State, the Christian influence has prevailed in American government since its infancy. It shows up, literally, on American currency, on the walls of the Washington monument, the Capital dome, and in many other buildings and structures at the hub of democracy. It rings in the Pledge of Allegiance, the oath of citizenship, even in the opening rites of the High Court. But more especially this influence is mirrored in the virtuous spirit of the law. Indeed, ours is a legal structure which was built by Christians in accordance with the dictates of Christian principles.

How prudently our forefathers worked to author the foundational documents of our nation. The Declaration of Independence and the Constitution of the United States are living, working testimonials to their courage, insight, and unselfish heed for the well-being and prosperity of future generations.

This foundling new country grew to be one of the most successful, powerful, and respected nations in the world in a historically short period of time. Perhaps this rise to greatness can be attributed, at least in part, to the solid moral backbone of our founding government and the altruistic premise from which it was forged.

Then, on January 22, 1973, the Supreme Court ruled in favor of abortion on demand in the infamous Roe vs. Wade case. (For a more detailed look at Roe vs. Wade, refer to the following chapter.) This inofficious decision jaundiced the vitals of democracy with oblique and specialized interpretations of the law.

I refer specifically to the right to privacy conferred by the Fourteenth Amendment, which was somehow interpreted as the right of a woman not to be pregnant and so lawfully able to contract for the death of her unborn child.

Many argue that abortion is an implied Constitutional right, that akin to such privileges as freedom of speech, freedom of religion, freedom of press, should be freedom of "choice." Yes, indeed, I must agree that freedom of choice is a wonderful provision of our political administration. Among countless other liberties, one may choose whether or not to have sex, to use contraception, even to raise a child. When it comes to abortion, more befitting is the term "freedom to kill." And there is nothing in the writs of our Republic that would even suggest destroying innocent lives is an American right.

Legalists have confused victimization with responsibility. Instead of recognizing the responsibility they have for their bodies, they've declared women "victims" of unwanted pregnancies and so deserving of restitution. If I may restate an earlier thought — an individual freely chooses to have sex and if a child is conceived, he or she is a resultant, an indisputable consequence of a choice already made. A pregnancy can't be undone — only ended, either in birth, miscarriage, or abortion.

The halls of government failed to separate the real choice from the consequences of that choice.

No rhetoric can disguise the fact that abortion denies the child his or her right to life. To say the warped translation of the Fourteenth Amendment was unfortunate is a sweeping understatement. Its repercussions have been forced upon millions and millions of tiny children. Daily, hourly, minutely, American blood is spilled on American ground — by American citizens! Roe vs. Wade opened the floodgates to a deluge of wholesale destruction. It was a grave political blunder, the proverbial "wrong turn."

A most sagacious phrase in the Declaration of Independence reads: "Prudence indeed will dictate that Governments long established should not be changed for light and transient causes." Yet the Supreme Court of the U.S. negated this piece of wisdom when

103

it parted from a faithful understanding of the Constitution and handed down that fateful ruling.

Free abortion was launched in the wake of the rebellion and unrest of the 1960s as perhaps a compensating "sign of the times." It is interesting to note that the Fourteenth Amendment was ratified in 1866 and this new interpretation wasn't made for over 100 years. Those federal justices took the path of least resistance in the face of a social temper tantrum as they bereaved our unseen citizens of the right to life. It seems, at least with this transient cause, the Court's judgment was more cowardly than supreme.

And abortion-mania is indeed transient. It is incorrectly assumed that most Americans favor legal abortion. Yet, according to a recent poll of some 50,000 high school students, the percentage that supports legal abortion is down from 70% twelve years ago to 46% today. Similar studies of married women indicate that three out of four "wouldn't even consider" abortion as an option when faced with an unplanned pregnancy. Other polls conducted on diverse groups nationwide disclose paralleled results.

Could it be the graceless fallacy of Roe vs. Wade is losing its transient luster?

Fairness, equality, and opportunity are qualities synonymous with "America." The Statue of Liberty stands in New York's harbor, an avatar of these principles. A beacon of refuge, she symbolizes the promise of a better life for the poor, the persecuted, and the oppressed. Her heartening proclamation to all who journey to this land is, "This is America. You are welcome here."

This is not to say that our recent history has been a model utopia. Indeed, we have struggled with immanent strife and lingering prejudices. Many subcultures and ethnic or economic minorities had been denied operative equality for too long. However, even though we may still be in a period of amends, we are endeavoring to practice what we as a nation stand for in theory — to live up to the words "of the people, by the people, for the people."

Quite distinctly at variance with this is the Roe vs. Wade decision which has imposed certain unlikely and unfixed specifications to qualify for "personhood." Lawful abortion contravenes the mores of a civilized, equable people. It hopelessly belies the historical precedent set by our nation — a precedent recognizing that all men are created equal (not born equal), and that it is from God (not the government) that we inherit our rights as human beings. This precept is eloquently put forth in the Declaration of Independence: "We hold these truths to be self-evident, that all men are created equal, that they are endowed by their creator with certain unalienable rights, that among these are life, liberty, and the pursuit of happiness. That to secure these rights, governments are instituted among men deriving their just powers from the consent of the governed."

So, it is to the law that citizens must ultimately turn for protection of their divinely appointed immunities. I hasten to add that the particulars of civil rule are but a guideline of proper conduct sanctioned by a collective conscience. Cogent law must begin within the individuals of the governed population. Regulations forbidding murder will be of little use to a helpless victim staring up the barrel of a gun held by a homicidal maniac. Likewise, a drug addict thirsting for a chemical "high" probably won't stop to consider the anti-drug laws before shooting up.

The law must have conscionable meaning within each person to be totally effectual.

So, it is in our hearts that we must first come to realize the injustice of abortion. Only then can we turn to our legal system to reinstate the ousted rights of our unborn American citizens. Until popularly understood law and the complex of moral principles which governs humans internally are united in essence and direction, we will be forced to live with the deficiencies of the present mode of government.

Who Decides When Life Begins?

Q: Do you believe in abortion?
A: Definitely.

Q: At anytime during the pregnancy?

A: Oh, no! Up until about 3 months.

Q: Why 3 months?

A: Well, because it starts to become a baby after that — it's alive.

Q: So, if I conceived on August 10th, you'd see nothing wrong in my having an abortion up to the 10th of November?

A: Right. That's your option.

Q: What if I waited until the 11th?

A: Well, one day doesn't make that much difference.

Q: Oh, OK. How about five days? How about the 15th?

A: Uh, well, it'd probably be OK.

Q: Could I stretch it out to the 25th? Or the 30th?

A: I think it would start to bother me at that point.

Q: Oh. Well, let's back up and try and pinpoint the exact time you feel the being becomes a baby. When is that transition? Maybe on the 17th at 2:30 p.m.? Or perhaps on the 20th at noon?

A: Uh. . . .

Just when does a developing baby enter the ranks of human-hood? This question must be the center of any serious discussion of abortion. And there is only one answer for pro-lifers.

However, such a diversity is found in the beliefs of abortion supporters that we can further categorize them: those who become opposed to abortion at three months gestation; at four months; at quickening, at six months, and so on. And let's not forget those few who, without compunction, support a woman's right to abort up until the day of natural delivery. The key phrase, "become opposed," indicates the flimsy structure of the person's belief which is subject to change at will.

How foolish it seems to try and pinpoint the moment of "first life" or "ensoulment" in a being that has been developing steadily and resolutely since the initial fusion of parent cells. Equally fatuous is how this pivotal moment can change from person to person or from circumstance to circumstance. Apparently, it is a matter adjustable to convenience and lifestyle.

Proponents of abortion have come to be stultified by a tendency to deny the continuity of the life cycle. In their refusal to accept conception as life's obvious beginning, they entangle themselves in the inanity of the "magic moment" syndrome. They choose to believe that a fertilized ovum is not a person but that a newborn baby is — which means that somewhere during that 38-week stretch, meaningful life must "catch up" with the growing being. When is the "magic moment"? At what point is there a sudden metamorphosis from protoplasm to child?

Here lies the cardinal flaw in the pro-abortion argument. Propped by hollow rhetoric, it cannot bear the impossible onus of having to differentiate between the nature and vibrancy of life at one point of gestation and at any immediately successive stage. It hasn't the faculty to address the simple truth that the child at one hour of age is the same child three months later. And six months after that. And for always.

And, God help us, if it is wrong to kill him or her at five months, it is just as wrong to kill this same individual two months earlier.

On Planned Parenthood Propaganda

In 1963, Planned Parenthood made this statement: "An abortion kills the life of a baby after it has begun. It is dangerous to your life and health. It may make you sterile so that when you want a child you cannot have it." [13]

As we look back upon these words, it seems Planned Parenthood was a fair-weather friend to the unborn children. Some time ago it shed this peaceful philosophy for an almost craven worship of abortion. It was involved in the litigation which unloosed this billow of death upon us. Today, publications of the organization refer to pregnancy as an "illness" that "has many characteristics of the conventional v.d. (venereal disease)." [14]

Planned Parenthood has become the vanguard in the war on the unborn, erecting an army of clinics nationwide for dispensing contraceptives and sex education materials and for providing abortions or referrals for abortions. With the number increasing every year, now nearly 100,000 human beings are destroyed annually under the aegis of Planned Parenthood.[15]

The influence of the organization is vast in scope. Planned Parenthood and its affiliates serve millions of women each year in various capacities, staff over 20,000 paid workers and volunteers, and lecture frequently at schools and community groupings. They receive tens of millions of dollars annually from government sources alone. Private contributions and clinic income yield additional monies.

In a self-defining excerpt from one of its brochures, Planned Parenthood calls itself ''A private, non-profit organization that provides confidential family planning, medical counseling, and educational services.'' Its philosophy is portrayed as wholesome, compassionate, and ''pro-family.'' Its advertisements, circulars, and slogans work to further its public mien as a good, serviceable part of the health-care community.

Yet one can't help but question the integrity of a group with such irresolute goals and renegade intentions. If it could change from guardian to adversary of the unborn, what might lie ahead on its itinerary? One of Planned Parenthood's most visible posters promises to strive for the day when ''every child will be a wanted child.'' What, precisely, does that mean? There is no mention of age, physical or mental capabilities, family income, social status.

With this vague slogan as its motto, and in light of its past history of fickle dedication, is it unreasonable to wonder if Planned Parenthood might next condone the elimination of all unwanted children?

On the Pervading Presence of the Media

They come into our homes every day. They might have breakfast or supper with us or even put us to sleep at night. Whether or not they always have a direct impact on us, the receivers, is debatable. The influence is there, though, perhaps stored away in the recesses of the mind, or perhaps coming about indirectly through one of the millions of others who, daily, watch, listen, or read. They are the media.

The ascendancy of the media, television in particular, their capacity to educate, inform, reshape the way we think, sway our opinions, even unite in times of crisis, is a power that cannot be overstated.

Public opinion and mood are, in significant measure, at the mercy of electronic transmittances. Remember how visual depictions of the emaciated Ethiopian people ignited a contagion of shock and galvanized a country to action. Recall the Challenger tragedy. During the hours and days after the explosion in space the almost nonstop coverage of the disaster tugged at the heartstrings of a nation.

That advertising executives and manufacturers constantly reap the benefits of the media sway points out how valuable a few seconds of air time can be.[16] Turn this few seconds into five hours daily and multiply by millions of people and you have an unparalleled force of persuasion and communication.

So, the influential prowess of the media lies not only in their sensuous presentation and delivery but also in their almost ubiquitous reach. At least one television set can be found in 85 million American households. The children of today clock more time in front of the TV than they do in the classroom. Adults, too, spend more of their spare hours soaking up the rays of the "tube" than they do any other single activity. Radios, newspapers, and periodicals, also, are universally popular.

Inevitably, the abortion mentality has permeated these powerful public agencies, too. And to what end?

On television, more and more often soap operas, movies, dramas, even situation comedies are broaching the subject of abortion. One character on a highly rated prime-time serial referred to having an abortion as flippantly as one might mention going to the hairdresser. Try as I might, I couldn't detect a hint of regret or sadness or any form of emotion for that matter. Ending her "pregnancy" was simply an easy and logical solution to an inopportune "accident."

Another show, a situation comedy, dedicated two full programs to the dilemma of its leading lady and her untimely pregnancy. And while the show offered different points of view regarding the abortion issue, the ''child'' was destroyed, prompting right-to-life demonstrations and boycotts of the network's affiliates.

My friends, abortion is not funny.

Admittedly, sitcoms have a history of levity and a broader base of subject matter available now than ever before, but I must maintain that the killing of unborn innocents against a laugh track defies understanding.

In yet another situation comedy, a long-married couple with grown children was suddenly faced with an unplanned pregnancy. The two discussed the pros and cons of having a child at this stage of life as if the baby didn't yet exist. It was clear that their ultimate decision to ''have a baby'' was not based on goodwill toward the living human already growing in her womb but rather on their realization that they could ''make room'' for the child in their lives. What a golden opportunity was missed to show how a devoted family can accept, unhesitatingly, a little ''surprise package,'' without deliberating matters of practicality and interruption of lifestyle.

There have been television movies in which women have died from the physiological complications of abortions, although clearly they couldn't be labeled ''pro-life.'' Their plots underscored the desperate straits and hardships of unwed motherhood in a way that made abortion seem the only ''answer.''

Women in other films have suffered no physical or emotional aftereffects.

Somewhere in between these two visionary extremes lies most of the real world. Meanwhile, the pseudo-realism of fictional TV continues to show us how abortion fits into the lives of everyday people, how it ''solves'' certain problems, how its availability and allure stretch from the frightened young teenager to the affluent middle-aged socialite, how this life-or-death matter can be discussed like contact lenses or yesterday's stew.

Sadly, the intentions of anti-abortionists are subject to misrepresentation by television fiction, too. Often, TV feeds the myth of the "typical" pro-lifer as a puritanical judge with a Bible in one hand and a bomb in the other.

It's appropriate that the most convincing cases of pro-life programming are not the products of a writer's imagination but rather the marvels of the natural world. One such presentation, aptly titled "The Miracle of Life," is seen on the P.B.S. series NOVA. Through electron microscopy and probes, the inner workings of the human reproduction systems are visually portrayed on the screen. We journey with the sperm on their perilous mission to find and fertilize the mature human egg, and finally witness firsthand the delicate beauty of the growing child. A writer on his best day couldn't manufacture a more sensitive or persuasive piece of work for the pro-life cause than has nature herself.

Another real-life drama, "The Silent Scream," shows an ultrasound image of a twelve-week fetus during an actual abortion. This powerful program cuts through the "between the woman and her doctor" claptrap and reveals the other side of abortion — where someone else is involved.[17]

The news media, which pride themselves on their objective analysis and presentation of daily events and local, national, and world affairs, are not immune to bias on the abortion issue either. I remember one radio newsman who, while broadcasting the local morning news, injected this personal remark: "I've always thought a woman has the right to her own body," and then proceeded to do an abortion-related story. That unsolicitated and unprofessional commentary brought a rash of letters to the station's management.

Another reporter, on the late evening edition, let her predilection for abortion all but glow during a television interview.

Although the percentage of abortion supporters among newspeople is high, it seems to be only the small local stations who may occasionally display an open bent for the pro-abortion cause. It has been my observation that, overall, network coverage of this tempestuous issue has been painstakingly fair-minded, particularly during the last few years. Both sides receive equal time and reporters and interviewers remain guardedly removed from the public fray.

Still, for an event that occurs thousands of times daily and touches so many lives, abortion receives relatively little press. It is a rare occasion that abortion is explored sensitively or covered at length. In fact, seemingly the only time the matter of killing the unborn even makes the news is when some type of legislation is being bounced about in Congress or when there are threats or violence to abortion clinics. Once in a while a case going to court involving a father trying to save his child from death will be aired. Political campaigns and anniversary marches also occasion cursory mention of this controversial issue — but even in all of these "newsworthy" stories, the principal focus is on distal points and not on the actual crime of abortion itself. Long forgotten and never mentioned are the children who die. Just once I'd like to hear a newscast open like this: "It is estimated fifty people died nationwide today in traffic accidents involving alcohol and 4,000 children lost their lives in abortions."

I can remember, as a young child, my astonishment at seeing ads for divorces. "Quick divorce, $50.00" or "Undisputed divorces, $75.00 and up." It was difficult to understand how the institution of marriage, which is supposedly based on love, friendship, and trust, could be so belittled, and how people could, so unabashedly, cash in on the difficulties of the marital partnership. Today, many newspapers and local television and radio stations have accepted the role of marketing tool for the commodity of abortion as advertisements of services to kill the unborn frequent these forums. We see and hear, "Pregnant? Need help? Call us." or "Free abortion counseling" or "Unwanted pregnancy? Abortion fees on sliding scale. Confidential." In the feeling heart, murder on the open market kindles a deep sense of bewilderment and sadness.

The media are not out to canonize abortion. The incidents and observations noted are not strategies in some pro-abortion plan of media menticide. However, they may be making the "fit" just a little easier.

That's why each comment like that of the radio personality,

every TV program, novel, or article that glamorizes abortion or at least makes it seem the only natural solution in certain situations, each ad for killing the unborn nestled comfortably between ads for Coke and Chevrolet, numbs the conscience of a growingly insensate population and allows legal abortion to settle a little deeper into the niche it has found for itself in our society.

Summary

"You will wake up on the count of three," the hypnotist told the volunteer, "and you'll feel fine — except you will forget the number six. It will become completely nonexistent."

Upon "three," the volunteer emerged from his trance. The hypnotist asked him to count his fingers. Of course without the number six the volunteer counted eleven fingers.

"Eleven?" the hypnotist scoffed. "How many fingers have you on your left hand?"

The volunteer counted and replied "five."

"And on your right?" Again, the volunteer counted and answered "five." "What are five and five?" asked the hypnotist.

"Ten" the volunteer answered, growing more and more perplexed.

"Then how can you possibly have eleven fingers? Count them again!"

Once more counting eleven fingers, the volunteer was visibly frustrated.

If there is a lesson tucked away in this episode, perhaps it might be that the omission of one bit of reality from a way of thinking can disrupt the entire process.

The piece of information rebuffed in the abortion mentality is the life and worth of the unborn child. That is our number six. Without it things just don't "add up." This chapter has offered a peek at what the exclusion of this fact has meant to society at large. We've seen the vacillating "principles" of the abortion mentality, the recurring inconsistencies of thought patterns. We've surveyed the havoc and disorder generated within all aspects of society, most notably the legal imperium, which holds as a right that which squelches rights, and the medical community which extols as remedial that which propagates death.

But the ugly effects of the mentality are with us, too, in far more subtle ways. Pitting unborn baby against the convenience of the mother, the mentality has forever altered the parent/child relationship. Today children grow up knowing they could have been robbed of life at their mother's request. What long-range influences this may have on the growing child remains to be seen. Is such an awareness supposed to make the youngster feel good? Should the child rejoice that he or she was among the 75% or so of the unborn who "made it" to the outer world? Or, can it come back to haunt him or her, particularly if older or younger siblings succumbed to abortion? Especially in times of hardship or failure will the thought come, "Maybe it would have been better if I had been aborted"? Might the child speculate on his or her ability to "live up to" this privilege of life bestowed by the parents?

I know a mother who begged her unwed daughter to have an abortion when the young woman found herself unexpectedly pregnant. The daughter refused and bore a beautiful son. Today, about two years later, that child is adored by his grandmother! He is the most precious thing in her world. How does she deal with the fact that she once pleaded for his death?

And what about the *eclectic* dimension? Eclectic is an adjective which means "choosing what appears to be the best from diverse sources." Each year tens of thousands of parents opt to abort a defective baby, many of whom already have children. Imagine what might pass through these little minds. The mentality has engendered an environment wherein a child might ask, "Mom, if you would've discovered I was handicapped, would you have aborted me?" or "Mom, what would you do to me now if I suddenly became crippled or deaf or very sick? Would you still want me? Would you still love me?"

These unsavory connotations are with us precisely because the abortion ethic says not wanting one's children is perfectly okay. The unborn are relegated to the ever-widening twilight zone between the light of "meaningful life" and the dark of "non-life." Here, definitions are sculpted, not by the fine hands of truth but by personal intent and purpose. Parental attitudes are the yardstick of a child's worth and the litmus indicator of his or her ultimate earthly disposition.

Can we live amid this rising tide of dishonesty without measurable effect on ourselves? Hardly.

The victims of the abortion mentality number far more than the 1.5 million babies killed each year. They are the parents of these babies, many of whom battle feelings of guilt and shame and all of whom must bear the incredible burden of living with this act of death.

They are those in direct complicity. A good number of pro-abortion legislators, doctors, and counselors pack thousands of deaths on their consciences.

And there are the rest of us. It is we who must buffet the far-reaching effects of abortion on demand. It is we who must live in the fallout of perfunctory murder.

When we can exist day by day with nary a prayer or word of protest on behalf of the unborn, we suffer, too, with the effects of prolonged exposure to the abortion mentality. And it is highly infectious. Our children might inherit this acquiescence to murder. Our friends and neighbors are likely to "catch it." To be sure, passive acceptance is a transgression that indurates the heart and soul of society to abortion at a rate only slightly slower than active endorsement. Let there be no doubt we are smitten with the full requital of silence and apathy.

Our number six has vanished from sight, though it has not escaped the grip of the heart. For, even after millions of abortions and years of legal sanction, something still doesn't "seem right." There remains a malaise, a compelling strain of secrecy and shame with respect to abortion.

A large part of a psychiatrist's work involves helping patients deal with unresolved conflicts and repressed traumas. He knows that when left to fester in the subconscious mind these troubles may surface later in curious, often detrimental ways.

In a much broader sense, the discord of abortion has rankled the social mind for years. We cannot flee the scions of the abortion ethic. They surface unsparingly.

If we are to regain a state of moral equilibrium, free from the mercurial rationale of the abortion mentality, we need rediscover the life and worth of the unborn. We must find our lost number six and, having done this, restore it irrevocably to its proper place in the grand equation of life.

The question remains — what can we do? Perhaps only after examining the sociogenetic factors that have evoked this trend of destruction can we begin to know how to work toward its banishment. This is the task of the upcoming chapter.

CHAPTER SIX

Meeting
the Challenge
of Abortion

Abortion is the leading cause of death in the U.S. Each year it claims more lives than heart attacks, cancer, or automobile accidents. Twenty-four hours a day, 365 days a year, abortion kills an unborn child every 18 seconds. In 15 days' time, more babies are lost than were Americans in the Vietnam War.

Just what has brought us to this point? The answer, I fear, is far too complex for an instant analysis. However, certain shifts of the social temperament invite mention in these pages. I hesitate to call them changes because they are not necessarily new to this era. Rather, they are more like tendencies or traits which have been intensified and magnified in this fast-paced, technology-happy time in history.

The Breeding Ground

Please keep in mind that the four following assertions are inductions of a most general nature, affording only an overview of the cultural tide. They are not put forth with the design of lumping everyone together into one preconceived category.

The *first trait* is an overall diminished regard for human life. We live in a time when the success and power of a nation is measured, at least in part, by the sophistication of its martial weaponry and by the number of people it can destroy. What meaning does a single human life have when we can boast of the ability to kill millions with the mere push of a button?

Worldwide riots sparked by racial or religious prejudice or political unrest, acts of terrorism, and senseless violence abound. With all of the "illegal" killing on the streets (for money and drugs and bigotry and jealousy, or for the "thrill of it"), and the "legal" killing of war (for supreme reign, for national boundaries, for God!?), regard for human life often takes a back seat to other issues.

Of course grim stories of wars have filled the pages of our history books for a long time. Neither casualties of international conflict nor street-killing are unique to this age. However, it seems that as the number of people being killed (or capable of being killed) steadily rises, so, proportionately, does concern for the individual falter.

This is not to say concern no longer exists. Violence and death on a worldscale, particularly when the media feeds it to us daily, are difficult for the average person to absorb. So, if after a while people harden to human suffering, it is perhaps an inner defense mechanism, like an emotional "shock absorber" that triggers such a response.

The *second trait* has to do with the pursuit of the "easy life." If we look around our homes most of us will see numerous gadgets and appliances assigned to simplify our daily routines. The market appeal and eventual success of any new product hinges largely on its time-saving and effort-saving capabilities.

Not so long ago automobiles, telephones, refrigerators, and other appliances, even hot and cold running water, were not everyday household particulars. Today we can pop dinner into the microwave or self-cleaning oven and control the temperature of our homes with the turning of a dial. We use disposable diapers, disposable plates, disposable lighters and watches. Our shelves are lined with instant potatoes, instant coffee, instant pudding, instant breakfast. We have machines that wash and dry clothes, do the dishes, and provide entertainment.

Generally, we are a people unschooled in patience, ever seeking an "easier way." Ruminations on this needn't all be unfavorable. There are positive sides to this standard of living, one being that more time can be given to important matters with the elimination of many tedious and trivial tasks. However, this thirst for easy solutions or instant gratification may take the form of self-indulgence, especially as it crops up in inappropriate facets of the decision-making process.

Too often we tend to seek solutions that will afford us the least amount of bother at the time. Caught up in an accelerated pace of life, we like the shortest route and often don't give proper heed to long-term consequences. No doubt the alarming number of alcoholics and drug abusers in our nation are searching for quick relief from the tensions and pressures of life. Many allege that the escalating rate of divorce is another sequel to the "easy way out" syndrome.

The *third trait* is the emergence of a casual, quite self-absorbed generation.

We have been instructed to keep this commandment: "Love one another. As I have loved you, so you also should love one another" (John 13:34).

How many of us actually love so unconditionally that we are willing to die for others, as our Lord did for us? This brand of love may seem a rare thing, yet God exemplifies its power continually in what is perhaps the purest, most selfless love on earth — that of parent for child. It is in this bond that we can come to know the sheer strength of his love for us and the supreme sacrifice it was for him to watch his only Son suffer and die.

How sadly ironic, then, that parents dispose of the children of their own flesh for wholly selfish reasons. Indeed they may convince themselves and others that such action is out of concern for their offspring. The soul of true love holds no place for such mental disarray.

Coined in the 60s, the popular phrase "looking out for Number One" capsulizes a self-interested approach to living that continues in force today.

The *fourth and final trait* consists of new attitudes and changing lifestyles which brought on more pregnancies. Even with available birth control methods we find ourselves confronting more and more "unwanted" or "careless" pregnancies. Several reasons might be held accountable. Among these is the rise in sexual activity among teens. The plunge into the domain of physical intimacy is happening at younger and younger ages. Today it is not at all uncommon for a twelve or thirteen-year-old to be sexually active. (Thirty-eight percent of all teens who become pregnant opt for abortion.)

Another contributing factor is, simply, that there are more women of childbearing age — up about one third since the early 70s. Yet annually more than twice the number of children as in 1973 are subjected to the private holocaust of abortion chambers (a disproportionate 100% increase!). One may be led to deduce that it's not a "big deal" to become pregnant anymore since it's a predicament easily remedied. Again we see the cycle of death that legal abortion perpetuates.

A final factor might be that no longer is the stigma of marital status a crucial factor in the considerations of pregnancy. Unwed motherhood is even thought to be quite "fashionable" in some circles, a proclamation of independence and self-possession.

Although the elimination of this taboo could, in theory, decrease the number of abortions, pregnancies out-of-wedlock still account for 75% of all legal abortions.

There we have it. These traits: more careless pregnancies, less regard for human life, an overriding emphasis on "me," and a society that endorses quick and easy solutions, have proved to be a fertile breeding ground for abortion mania.

But, can we not see that the "solution" of abortion addresses only the most superficial needs of a society grown restive? If a piece of glass were to become lodged in someone's foot, would it be better to administer a pain-killer or to remove the glass?

It might be said that legal abortion is a large-scale "pain-killer," assuaging the most obvious "symptoms," yet all the while perpetuating a need for itself by overlooking the source of those symptoms.

Here, finally, is where we should direct our attention and energies to combat this mass addiction to the narcotic, abortion. For if we are effectively to flush this tide of corruption from the social scene, we must quiet its dictatorial hold on us. So imperative it is that we first become sensitive to the deeper needs of ourselves as a people that all other efforts to deal with the problem prove futile. We must look to the source of our troubles, confront them at their genesis so that we might search out a solution of lasting benefit — one with which all can live.

Sweeping Court Decisions

Although the practice of abortion was morally and religiously impermissible for many centuries (especially after quickening when primitive "science" believed the baby instantaneously came to life), it had only been forbidden by secular law since the period around 1870. During this post-Civil War era, a nation was awakened to human and civil rights issues. It was at this time the Thirteenth and Fourteenth Amendments were voted into the Constitution, abolishing slavery. The "realm of personhood" and the rights and privileges of persons were expanded to include everyone, even slaves, who, just eleven years before, had been declared "property." The Fourteenth Amendment also proclaims: "No state shall make or enforce any laws which shall abridge the privileges or immunities of citizens of the United States; nor shall any state deprive any person of life, liberty, or property without due process of law, nor deny to any person within its jurisdiction the equal protection of the laws."

Concurrently, while these legal reforms took place, the scientific world was approaching a new awareness of human fertilization looming on the horizon. With increasingly more efficient microscopes and other technical equipment, much of the mystery, speculation, and myth that had surrounded conception since its correlation with intercourse was realized was finally eliminated. The scope of understanding would continue to broaden during the following one hundred years so that today we possess such a panoramic knowledge of early fetal development there is little doubt among the distinguished men and women of science that life exists from the moment of conception. More information uncovering the intricate activities of the intrauterine cosmos has been garnered during the past few decades than during centuries before.

It would seem only right, in light of these scientific findings, that governing law would continue to protect and defend unborn children with conviction proportionate to this new erudition. Is that what happened? No, during the five years prior to 1973, fourteen states had adopted a policy of legal abortion on request with very few restrictions. Then, on January 22, 1973, the Supreme Court, in a seven to two decision, ruled in favor of abortion rights, invalidating abortion laws in Texas and Georgia and, by implication, overturning statutes in the other states. Legalized abortion was born in a murky paradox, not ''in light of'' but ''in spite of'' decades of an ongoing and long overdue human and civil rights movement (which grew especially intense in the 60s), and in the face of clear, undeniable evidence of life beginning at conception.

As is inherently characteristic of representative government, a microscopic percentage of the whole (Congressmen, judges, etc.) ultimately legislate standards and set precedents that must be endured by us all. Insular court cases and specific individuals can carve permanent political channels.

So, while sweeping shifts in the attitude of the general populace may indeed be present, what tangible steps are taken to accommodate them or how justice is dispensed is contingent upon the disposition of the current political mesh.

The power of the individual in governmental function is very apparent. With a single statistic the gravity of the Roe vs. Wade decision can be gauged: Seven men are accountable for the deaths of 20,000,000 babies to date. That our legal system would allow a handful of people to carry the weight of so many lives on the basis of a solitary decision is frightening. Even more regretful is that these same power-laden individuals bared such a blind spot in their vision of justice.

Unless the Court reverses its decision, which is unlikely, only through a federal amendment to the Constitution can repatriation for the unborn become a reality.

One such proposed human life amendment basically promulgated that "person," as used in the Constitution, included the unborn and restated that no person shall be deprived of life. Simply, this would have nullified the 1973 decision and restored state authority as in the pre-Roe vs. Wade era. However it failed to pass by eighteen votes.

During the past fourteen years or so there have been several attempts, some successful, to dilute the potency of the Roe vs. Wade ruling, including the famous Hyde Amendment.

Although several pro-life bills passed in the House, they failed to pass in the Senate. The state legislators have fared somewhat better. Their efforts were mildly productive when, in 1977, the Supreme Court ruled that neither the Social Security Act nor the Constitution prevented a state from limiting the number of abortions performed under the Medicaid program. (But in November, 1986, the High Court decided states may not discontinue payments to private groups because they offer abortion services.)

The Court also ruled that a city may refuse to permit abortions in city hospitals that are publicly funded.

The list goes on and on. But while the battle rages within the halls of justice, babies keep on dying.

We can't let ourselves be satisfied with partial victories and incomplete reforms. For until abortion is banned altogether, the challenge of a lifetime stretches before us.

The Challenge of Truth

Truth is a challenge. It is a challenge because it can bring upon us painful awareness and sacrifice and reminds us of the necessity of dealing with realities we'd rather not face. It means taking things as they are — not as we'd like them to be. How readily we would change what is real if only we could do so and recast it to our own purposes and needs!

One truth stands solid and unfading, readily perceived by those who are open to it and easily found by those who seek it: Human life, in its many forms, is sacred beyond justifiable intervention, and abortion destroys such life.

Painful is this realization for it might mean coming to terms with a past endorsement of abortion or long-term indifference, both of which sting under truth's light. It means understanding exactly what abortion is to an unborn baby, feeling the agony right along with him or her. It means mourning new destinies, futures, and dreams hurled into oblivion.

So painful it is that some come to an acceptance of this truth reluctantly. They are carried there kicking and screaming, no longer able to resist its overpowering draw. Others, content in a shadowy existence, never arrive there at all.

Quite certainly it is more than just chance that untold millions of women lament over past abortions, yet how many are bitterly sorry they gave birth? Likewise, a growing number of private individuals and public figures, once staunchly pro-choice, are now unfettered enthusiasts of the pro-life cause. In turn, how many pro-lifers have openly and enthusiastically converted to pro-abortionism? I know of none. Still, all of us have to be wary of the insidious influence of the pro-abortion mentality that surrounds us on all sides. The steady inhaling of these noxious fumes has to take its toll. Numbness can take over, the urgency of the cause can begin to escape us, or discouragement about the monumental task ahead can debilitate us. Being tenaciously pro-life is an extraordinary challenge. It asks an enormous price in effort and dedication. It is seeing a need to change, then acting upon it.

Perhaps it is wrong to allege the evils of abortion without, at the same time, offering a solution to the problem of unwanted pregnancies.

To be certain, no secret remedy awaits us.

It is a complex situation that has been long in the developing. We can't expect it to disappear tomorrow or next week or next month. Profound change comes neither quickly nor easily. It is a process which unfolds only slowly and arduously.

The first essential to positive growth — the primary element in human healing — is love. Love takes root in the heart, fed on information, faith, and a sincere desire to help those in need.

Never to be forgotten is that every abortion has a human side. Women who choose to terminate their pregnancies are not callous monsters. Often they are frightened and confused and do a good deal of soul-searching before making their decision. Relatives or counselors may be pressuring them to abort. Financial difficulties and familial stress often enter the picture. We must not sit in judgment on them; rather we should be prepared to offer compassion, hope, and practical help.

Being pro-life means being pro-all life. This includes, in a special way, women who are distressed by pregnancy. It recognizes the fact that an expectant mother's problems don't begin with pregnancy nor will they end with abortion, and that inwardly she cries for something more than a violent end to her baby's life.

Many organizations nationwide are equipped to provide baby clothing and furniture, referrals to health-care and legal professionals, temporary housing and, perhaps most importantly, friendship, support, and a listening ear. In essence, they are there to make her life easier and more comfortable as she faces motherhood.

For those who feel unable to meet the demands of a small baby, placing the child is another alternative. Of course adoption comes with its own set of emotional drains on the mother. Relinquishing a child calls for a tremendous amount of courage. But how much better it is to give up a newborn to loving adoptive parents (and there are thousands in waiting) than to surrender him or her to death!

I've heard it said that abortion is preferable to the "unnatural" act of giving away one's own baby and that only an "unfit" mother would do such a thing. On the contrary — what could be as unnatural as to commission the death of one's own child? And nothing is more natural for a mother than to feel unselfish love for her little one, to want the best life possible for him or her. Three beautiful members of my family are adopted and I thank God their biological mothers were so "unfit."

Four Mind-sets and Six Steps to Meet the Challenge

Reverence for life is not a part-time duty, to be defended only when conditions suit us. It has to be, of itself, a total, ever-renewing inner commitment, alive in the very bosom of daily existence. Here are four mind-sets to help you meet this challenge:

Remember the uniqueness and the unrepeatable treasure of each individual. Time after time Scripture alerts us to the importance of the individual in the scheme of humanity.[1] You and I, too, are among these priceless ones — singles which cannot be disengaged from the whole. And so are the as-of-yet unborn individuals, differing only in chronological placement.

Statistics can be so overwhelming as to be almost meaningless. We speak of 1.5 million children dying each year, yet the number is too large to contemplate.

When a powerful earthquake flattened a foreign city recently, the death toll ran into the thousands. The victims were nameless, faceless to us. Then, suddenly, the disaster was brought home. A national newscast showed a rescue worker pulling from the rubble the crumpled body of a small child. There it was — we saw the devastation, the loss of life, the pain. The tragedy became real.

Though we cannot perceive abortion's victims with our physical eyes, our hearts throb with the knowledge that each is an individual with vast potential. Each is special, real. Do not think in terms of 1.5 million per year. Think of that child that is being shredded alive NOW. Think of those who will silently writhe in pain before you finish reading this chapter. Concentrate on that young boy or girl who might be sleeping or sucking a thumb at this very moment while a doctor prepares the instruments which will pierce his or her tiny body.

Postpone instant gratification for the rewards of patience, endurance, and consistency of effort. The great lesson of life (and one that is difficult to master) is the discipline of patience. Seldom is anything of value gained in haste. Sometimes we discover the hard way that choices which bring pleasure or relief today prove the bane of tomorrow's happiness.

Love unselfishly. Learning to ignore selfish motives and to put the needs of others before our own is a directive which leaps from the pages of the New Testament. The great commandment, we are told, is to "love the Lord your God with your whole heart, with your whole soul, with your whole mind," and the second is like it, "love your neighbor as yourself."

Authentically selfless love endures and finds meaning in not only joyful times but the tribulations of human interaction which bore through a person's soul.

Remember, in loving your unseen neighbor you will be loving God himself who also escapes the reach of our physical sight. And in defending the persecuted you will be defending Christ himself who, too, met with oppression, disdain, torture, and finally death. "Whoever receives one child such as this in my name receives me" (Matthew 18:5).

Approach sexual relationships with caution. Know that sexuality is a multidimensional phenomenon, embracing much more than fleeting physical pleasure. The human sexual experience involves two whole persons, complete with emotions, needs, and vulnerabilities, and, at their communion, awaiting at a distance, is the possibility of new life.

These, in their common element of love, are directed at the inner person — to vitalize the meaning of the gift of life and to navigate the heart to peak sensitivity in its contemplation of this gift in all its variety.

From this base of moral solidarity springs a number of more tangible steps we can take to end the massacre in our midst.

Share your education regarding human conception and growth.

Amazingly, there is widespread misinformation about prenatal development — even among health-care professionals.

I spoke with one person, a trained ambulance attendant for many years and mother of five, who had witnessed a woman having a miscarriage in early pregnancy. She was astonished at the humanness of the perfectly formed child, but four or five inches long, which she held in her hand. "I couldn't believe it," she said to me, "the tiny arms and legs, all the veins beneath the skin. . . ." She, like a surprising many, had thought a child at that stage was more of a blob or an indistinct mass of tissue.

Along with the dissection of frogs, perhaps school biology curricula should devote more time to the study of the human animal as it develops in the womb.

Write letters. A letter can be an effective form of communication. Send your views to the editors of newspapers, magazines, and to elected officials. Don't exaggerate or sensationalize. You're likely to elicit more recognition and more action if you stick to the facts. Stay abreast of political issues and pending legislation by reading the newspaper and being on mailing lists. Write today. There is strength in numbers.

Get on the air. Radio and TV talk shows that welcome audience input also provide an ideal opportunity to speak out.

Support pro-life groups with donations of time, money, baby goods, or whatever else they may need. In doing so, you directly help those women who have chosen to keep their babies. You also provide the facilities that the groups need to continue their work and perhaps make it easier for other women to choose life for their children.

Vote pro-life. Make sure you understand a candidate's position on the abortion issue before you make your final decision at the polls.

Keep praying. Prayer and its power to transform are gifts which indwell us all. Every day, share this gift. Let love and concern for the unborn and their mothers fill your heart as you seek God. Thank him for revealing his truth to you and seek his guidance in your crusade to gain respect for unborn children. Ask for strength and perseverance to uphold your convictions through adversity and the venom of ridicule. Pray that your life might be a positive voice for the unborn and an instrument of his peace. Finally, pray for laws which will again reflect universal human worth.

A Letter of Love

Dear Friend,

Today you can legally abort your child, but what you cannot abort is the fact that this little one is your own flesh and blood and that, someday, you will meet him or her face-to-face.[2]

The crusade for an abortion-free society is long and difficult and one that cannot be won overnight. Impeding the way are those who tell us not to impose our beliefs on others when it is they, the followers of abortion, who publish the dictates of oppression. Remember that we are answerable only to God, not to the faulty judgments of humankind.

As previously mentioned, I believe the number of people who oppose abortion is much higher than most would think. Besides those who speak out, there are many ''closet'' pro-lifers who hesitate to do so in an age where it's not fashionable to be anti-abortion. However, the majority of pro-lifers are those who will voice the injustice of abortion to their family and friends, yet go no further. They do absolutely nothing, often feeling the entire predicament is hopeless and impossible to correct. And, ironically, it just may be without the momentum their help and outward support could provide.

Entombed in the notion that being pro-life is a hobby or pastime for a handful of activists, they don't see that assertive concern for our brothers and sisters, our sons and daughters, is an obligation and a responsibility incumbent upon us all. Never must we cease to feel one another's pain.

Those of us who know abortion is wrong — yet are resigned to inaction — must shoulder much of the blame for this sinful corruption that has overtaken us. Silence is deadly. "So for one who knows the right thing to do and does not do it, it is a sin" (James 4:17).

So, don't look to someone else as the force to change this process of death. You are uniquely prepared for the task. God has given you a gift to be shared — a gift that he gave to no one else. Accept this challenge to champion the pro-life cause. Wrap it snugly around your heart.

When our efforts seem unrewarded or, worse yet, unproductive, we must not lose faith. For sometimes it is when defeat seems imminent that victory is closest at hand.

Stained Hearts

Our first home's lush security
The warm confines of the womb
For some becomes a chamber of pain
And an early, violent tomb.

In the name of rightful convenience
Millions of children lie dead
Upon the hands of a few and the hearts of all
Their innocent blood is shed.

When we face God on that final day
How on earth will we explain
The undeniable presence
Of that incorrigible stain?

Conclusion

A statistical look at crime in the United States (compiled from "Crime in the United States," August 26, 1982, and "American Medical News"):

- A physically abused child dies every 105 minutes.
- A kidnapping takes place every 27 minutes.
- A murder occurs every 24 minutes.
- A forcible rape occurs every 7 minutes.
- An instance of aggravated assault happens once a minute.
- An unborn child dies in an abortion every 18 seconds.

Is this the legacy we want to bequeath to our children and grandchildren? Are we to be recorded in the annals of history as an age when legal murder exceeded all other violent crimes?

Another point to ponder: Will later generations look back upon this era in total disgust or will abortion be so widely practiced that they'll only laugh at our "primitive" techniques?

The acceptance of abortion in the future is not certain, though much of what is done today bears heavily upon this. However, the mechanics of the procedure itself will likely progress to a stage of peak efficiency and negligible discomfort and interruption of routine. A refined birth control pill or injection that can be taken days or weeks after conception might soon be the method of choice. What more could one ask for in an abortifacient than to be clean, easy, and safe for the mother?

As discussed in an earlier chapter, "cleaning up" abortion renders it no less ugly. In all probability, given the technological leaps of the recent past, abortion will be streamlined in the years to come. But whether the procedure yields a three-pound child-corpse or a microscopic human infant, the bottom line is that it takes a life.

If only we, who are caught in its bondage, could comprehend the creation of time. Would that we could know God sees us at once as a speck of life in our mother's womb and as an upright creature walking his earth.

The years of our mortal existence and the millennia before and after it are his to view in a single instant. The interim between conception and birth or conception and viability, upon which we place so much emphasis, is only "felt" by us.

With this understanding it is impossible to allow the repulsive meaning of abortion to dissolve into the comforts of progress.

How wonderful it would be if women could be pregnant or not at will — to have complete mastery over the reproductive process. But such is not the way of the world, much as we'd like it to be and strain to make it so.

In usurping the sage judgments of God and of nature we have visited the worst sort of turmoil upon ourselves. We have incurred a mountainous debt in this struggle for control: Each day brims with the deaths of thousands of innocent children. Millions have perished in the last two decades.

What possible earthly reparation can we offer for this? Does such an atonement exist? These little lives have been lost irretrievably, and with them all hope of amends in this world. No, we cannot repay this debt but we can seek forgiveness. Even for this grave liability, God stands ready to pardon anyone who seeks him with a repentant heart.

It has been a costly lesson, indeed. Let it not all be in vain. To resist the pedagogues of the past years now would truly be unforgivable.

There has been enough name-calling on both sides. The time has come for mutual understanding. In essence we all want the same thing — a resolution of the dilemma of unwanted pregnancies. The disunion between pro-life and pro-abortion forces is no more and no less than their perceptions of unborn life.

While pro-lifers uphold the sacredness of this life, pro-abortionists dismiss it as tissue, or, if as a life, then one that hasn't reached significance enough to outweigh maternal convenience. This schism forms an abysmal valley between the groups.

As pro-lifers, it is not our desire to be proved right. It is our desire to save babies from the dark hands of premature death.

Heaven knows, these are difficult times to raise children. Crime, drug abuse, illiteracy, and unemployment are national problems. Personally, there may be strained relationships, financial troubles, or physical and emotional abuse. But, God help us, there's a better solution out there — and it lies not in despair but in hope, not in conflict but in concern, not in death but in life.

How often our Father speaks of children as examples of grace. We are summoned to follow the lead of the children, to be as they are — in their unity of heart and unsullied wisdom; in their total dependence and trust; in their canny ways of seeing through to the truth; and in their inexhaustible reservoirs of awe and wonder at the world. These are the virtues which bring us to the feet of God and they are the compelling note on which to predicate our own faith.

Children are visits from the Almighty. Really, how unworthy we are to be the recipients of such magnificent gifts, yet still they are given to us. It is unspeakable that so many should be returned, abruptly and ungratefully, to the Giver.

My enduring hope is that we struggle against the false security of a rationale that would place the matter of managing life and death in the hands of mere mortal men and women. Until such time, until we as a nation, as a world, as children of God, welcome back the unborn into the fold of humanity, it is my fervent prayer that God might hold a very special place in heaven for these babies who were turned away from earthly life. Surely, he must.

A Child's Lead

Father, you told them one and all
that a child shall be their lead
But they hear not the sound of your bidding
oh, why do they not take heed?

Please, Father, the time is short
recount to them I plead
That the lifeblood of this dizzy world
flows behind a child's lead.

Afterword

And so it ends, with a challenge to be pro-life. And it truly *is* a challenge. Since 1973, society's acceptance of abortion has spread. Not individually, however. As this book quite rightly points out, the number of those *personally* opposed to abortion has grown. There are those "closet pro-lifers" who don't speak out because it is not chic, progressive, trendy, or liberal to be against "free choice." As a result we have blinded ourselves to the reality of the deaths occurring minute by minute, even as this page is written. It has become easier to stay silent, more acceptable to ignore, than to speak the truth. So the madness continues.

This is a disturbing book. It will not change the minds of those who are firmly in favor of abortion, for they have somehow learned to avoid dwelling on the inconsistencies and obvious contradictions of their position. Either that or they wholeheartedly accept social Darwinism in all its aspects. Human life must have no intrinsic value, no divine spark. Human life must only be valuable to the degree that it contributes to the general good or is specifically beneficial to a contributing member of society. Period. Social Darwinism is utilitarianism carried to an extreme. Only those who profess this viewpoint can be logically consistent in advocating abortion on demand. The rest of us should be very disturbed by the message just read, for it calls us to change, to confront the deceptions that we may have been living with.

For if we admit of any sanctity, any divine spark of human life, then we can come to no other conclusion than that abortion is the taking of one human life by another. In the chapter on fetal development, we read of the rapid development of the fertilized egg into the embryo and then into the fetus. There is only one "point of demarcation," where suddenly a distinctly unique human life appears. That moment is conception. Any other point is an arbitrary line dividing a smoothly flowing continuum. Some may argue for a later point, after the possibility of twinning has passed. Nevertheless, whether you have one or more distinct individuals, conception occurs when there is a distinction from the parents. New life has been engendered. The crux of the argument is found in the question, "Can doctors, lawmakers, or family members rightfully and in good conscience choose to end life because it may pose a threat to another?" I think we all know the answer to that one; life should only be taken in defense of life if there are no other alternatives.

Though I have never met Lori Van Winden, I know she has remarkable insight into the abortion issue in particular and our society as a whole. She has done a fine job revealing the tenuous constructs that the pro-abortion camp uses to support their claims. By appealing to the plight of the woman, the unseen true victim of abortion disappears. He or she becomes a "mass of cells," a "product of conception" (aren't we all?), or "undifferentiated tissue." Yet, it is the plight of the pregnant woman that keeps people from voicing their concerns about abortion. As Lori so aptly puts it, "Perhaps it is wrong to allege the evils of abortion without, at the same time, offering a solution to the problem of unwanted pregnancies. . . . In essence we all want the same thing — a resolution of the dilemma of unwanted pregnancies. The disunion between pro-life and pro-abortion forces is no more and no less than their perceptions of unborn life."

That is why the final chapter ends with a challenge. Lori challenges all of us. The committed pro-life activist must not give up, must not succumb to the allure of apathy and slide into a fog of indifference. Those less committed or less active should examine their motives for inaction. Is the fear of being on the ''wrong'' side of an issue worth continuing abortion on demand, worth the loss of life? It is a sad commentary on the value placed on human life that such a question need even be asked.

For all of us, this book is a call to conscience. If we do believe that human life is sacred, that it is a gift from God, then there can be no justification for any direct abortion. There are many unfortunate pregnancies, there are many unpleasant pregnancies, but abortion does not prevent pregnancy. As Planned Parenthood once stated, ''Abortion kills the life of the baby after it has begun.''

Kathryn Moseley, M.D.
Directory of Neonatology
Central Maine Medical Center
Lewiston, Maine

Notes

Preface
1. This statistic is for the United States alone. John F. Matthews, in "The Deadliest Profession,"*Human Life Review,* Spring, 1987, stated: "(T)he pro-abortion Alan Guttmacher Institute proudly announced last October that there were some 30 to 45 *million* legal abortions all around the world last year. (*Total* abortions are estimated at 55 million or more.)"
2. John T. Noonan, Jr., expressed the same idea in *A Private Choice: Abortion in America in the Seventies* (New York: Free Press, 1979), p. 1: "Once or twice in a century an issue arises so divisive in its nature, so far-reaching in its consequences, and so deep in its foundations that it calls every person to take a stand."

Chapter One
1. Geraldine Lux Flanagan, *The First Nine Months of Life* (New York: Simon & Schuster, 1962, 1965).
2. Lennart Nilsson, *A Child Is Born* (New York: Delacourt Press/ Seymour Lawrence, 1976; English copyright: Dell, 1966, 1977).
3. The calculations for the rate of growth from ovum to newborn as applied to the adult were figured for an 8-pound, 20-inch newborn and a 190-pound, 70-inch adult. The dimensions of the human egg (.005 inch) were obtained from Nilsson, *A Child Is Born,* p. 18, and (.00000005 oz.) from Theodosius Dobzhansky, *The Biological*

Basis of Human Freedom (New York: Columbia University Press, 1956), p. 13.

4. See "A Day in the Life of the Fetus" by Sir A. William Liley, M.D., in *New Perspectives on Human Abortion*, edited by T. Hilgers, D. Horan, and D. Mall (University Publications of America, 1981), p. 29: "As everyone knows, we each started life as a single cell. This single cell divided into two, the first generation of cell division; the two cells divided into four . . . and so on. And how many generations of cell division are required to produce the 30 billion cells which make up our adult bodies? The answer is about 45. Of these 45 generations of cell multiplication or replication, 8 have occurred by the time we implanted in the wall of our mother's uterus, 30 or nearly two thirds have occurred by 8 weeks' gestation, 38 have occurred by 28 weeks' gestation, 41 by the time we are born, and the remaining tedious 4 occupy the whole of childhood and adolescence. . . . It is obvious that in developmental terms we spend 90 percent of our lives *in utero,* and for some sensory and neural structures the percentage is even higher."

Chapter Two

1. J. C. Willke, with Mrs. Willke, *Abortion, Questions & Answers* (Cincinnati: Hayes Publishing Company, Inc., 1985), pp. 84-87.
2. Bernard Nathanson, with Richard Ostling, *Aborting America* (New York: Doubleday, 1979), pp. 45, 72-73, 273, 276.

Chapter Three

1. Donald Shoemaker, *Abortion, the Bible and the Christian* (Cincinnati: Hayes Publishing Co., 3rd printing, 1982).
2. P. Cameron, "How Much Do Mothers Love Their Children?" *Rocky Mountain Psychological Association,* May 12, 1972: "Most women who were most regretful of the pregnancy now claim they would have the child again if given the opportunity. . . . [The researchers concluded] . . . initial feelings about pregnancy are predictive of how a mother will eventually feel about her child to only a very limited degree."
3. Malcolm Muggeridge, "The Overpopulation Myth," *Human Life Review,* Spring, 1983, p. 117: "(T)here is also common sense, which tells us that if, for instance, the population of India were to be halved, as most of them are engaged in subsistence agriculture, there

would be half as much food available. In other words, the situation, as far as food supplies were concerned, would be unchanged."

4. See "Sexual Assault and Pregnancy," by Sandra Kathleen Mahkorn, M.D., and William V. Dolan, M.D., in *New Perspectives on Human Abortion,* edited by T. Hilgers, D. Moran, and D. Mall (University Publications of America, Inc., 1981), pp. 182-198. Also see "Abortion: The Hard Cases" (a leaflet, published by NRL Educational Trust Fund, Suite 402, 419 7th Street, N.W., Washington, D.C. 20004, (202) 638-4396).

5. *Roe vs. Wade,* U.S. Supreme Court, No. 70-18, p. 38, Jan. 1973.

6. Valerie Vance Dillon, *Nine Facts To Know About Abortion* (a pamphlet published by the Bishops' Committee for Pro-Life Activities, 1977).

7. John Lippis, *The Challenge To Be Pro-Life* (a pamphlet published by the Santa Barbara Pro-Life Education, Inc., 3rd ed., 1978).

8. Willke, *Abortion, Questions & Answers,* pp. 138-140.

9. Nathanson, *Aborting America,* pp. 235-236.

10. Willke, *Abortion, Questions & Answers,* pp. 208-209.

11. James Watson, "Children from the Laboratory," *AMA Prism,* May, 1973: "Because of the present limits of such detection methods, most birth defects are not discovered until birth. If a child were not declared alive until three days after birth, then all the parents could be allowed the choice . . . the doctor could allow the child to die if the parents so choose and save a lot of time and suffering."

12. Willke, *Abortion, Questions & Answers,* p. 162-167.

13. Nathanson, *Aborting America,* p. 193: "How many deaths were we talking about when abortion was illegal? In N.A.R.A.L. we generally emphasized the drama of the individual case, not the mass statistics, but when we spoke of the latter it was always '5,000 to 10,000 deaths a year.' I confess that I knew the figures were totally false, and I suppose the others did too if they stopped to think of it. But in the 'morality' of our revolution, it was a *useful* figure, widely accepted, so why go out of our way to correct it with honest statistics? The overriding concern was to get the laws eliminated, and anything within reason that had to be done was permissible."

14. See "The Beginnings of Personhood: Medical Considerations," by Andre E. Hellegers in *Perkins Journal* (Fall 1973): "In induced abortion it is the physician's action which causes the lack of viability. . . . The fact that an adult who cannot swim is not viable

hardly seems a sufficient justification for throwing him overboard and thus making him non-viable.''

15. See ''Preemies,'' in *Newsweek,* May 16, 1988.

Chapter Four

1. Lippis, *The Challenge To Be Pro-Life.*
2. Willke, *Abortion, Questions & Answers,* pp. 90-108.
3. Ann Saltenberger, *Every Woman Has a Right To Know the Dangers of Legal Abortion* (a pamphlet published by Air-Plus Enterprises, P.O. Box 367, Glassboro, N.J. 08028).
4. Willke, *Abortion, Questions & Answers,* pp. 119-127.

Chapter Five

1. Mary Meehan, ''Bishop Vaughan's Reasons,'' *National Catholic Register,* May 22, 1988: ''New York Auxiliary Bishop Austin Vaughan recently became the first Catholic bishop arrested for helping to block the entrance of an abortion clinic. . . . On May 1, the day before his arrest, he said: 'The longer you live with something that's bad alongside of you, the more you get used to it. I don't mean that you accept it or that you say it's all right. But you no longer get so excited. We have lived with that situation in our own country. . . . (W)e've reached a point where some say it's bad and some say it's good; but not much really happens to change the situation as it is. As long as that is, we're in a disaster that gets worse the longer it lasts.' ''
2. Adapted from: Willke, *Abortion, Questions & Answers,* pp. 226-228.
3. Willke, *Abortion, Questions & Answers,* p. 273.
4. Willke, *Abortion, Questions & Answers,* p. 196.
5. Dave Andrusko & Leslie Bond, ''More Medical Facilities Preparing to Make Jump Into Fetal Brain Transplants,'' in *National Right To Life News,* April 7, 1988.
6. Consider Shakespeare's *Richard the Third,* Act V. scene iv: ''A horse, a horse, my kingdom for a horse!''
7. For a documented study of the Holocaust/Abortion connection, see: James T. Burtchaell, *Rachel Weeping and Other Essays on Abortion* (Fairway, KS: Andrews and McNeel, Inc., 1982), pp. 141-238. Burtchaell found seven factors functioning both within Nazi Ger-

many and among today's American pro-abortion advocates. In both situations the practictioners:

1. depersonalized their victims,
2. euphemized their public and private vocabulary of death,
3. discharged responsibility for their acts onto others,
4. disavowed vicious intent,
5. once initiated, killed indiscriminately,
6. found it an occasion to acquire wealth,
7. were encouraged by a temporizing opposition.

8. "Baby Being Starved Under Court Decision," *San Francisco Chronicle,* April 15, 1982.

9. Willke, *Abortion, Questions & Answers,* p. 79: "Is abortion done for sex selection? Yes. And the girls are almost always the ones killed."

10. Willke, *Abortion, Questions & Answers,* p. 193: "Out of over 300,000 physicians in the U.S., there are about 8,700 who are willing to provide abortions."

11. Editorial, *Journal of the California State Medical Association,* September 1970: "The reverence of each and every human life has been a keystone of Western medicine, and is the ethic which has caused physicians to try to preserve, protect, repair, prolong, and enhance every human life.

"Since the old ethic has not yet been fully displaced, it has been necessary to separate the idea of abortion from the idea of killing, which continues to be socially abhorrent. The result has been a curious avoidance of the scientific fact, which everyone really knows, that human life begins at conception, and is continuous, whether intra- or extra-uterine, until death. The very considerable semantic gymnastics which are required to rationalize abortion as anything but taking a human life would be ludicrous if they were not often put forth under socially impeccable auspices. It is suggested that this schizophrenic sort of subterfuge is necessary because, while a new ethic is being accepted, the old one has not yet been rejected."

12. Nathanson, *Aborting America,* p. 268.

13. Willke, *Abortion, Questions & Answers,* pp. 286-287.

14. Willke, *Abortion, Questions & Answers,* p. 115.

15. Paul Marx and Judie Brown, *Facts About Planned Parenthood* (an informational sheet published by the American Life Lobby).

16. According to the November, 1986, issue of *Channels,* the average

30-second commercial (during regularly scheduled prime-time programming) cost $106,000. This paid for the air-time alone and did not include the production costs which were even greater.

17. For information about *The Silent Scream,* contact American Portrait Films, Suite 500, 1695 W. Crescent Avenue, Anaheim, CA 92801, (714) 535-2189. Recently Dr. Nathanson produced another pro-life film, *Eclipse of Reason.* For details, contact Bernadell, Inc., Dept. NRL, P.O. Box 1897, New York, NY 10011, (212) 463-7000.

Chapter Six

1. Shoemaker, *Abortion, the Bible and the Christian,* pp. 20-47.
2. Burtchaell, *Rachel Weeping and Other Essays on Abortion,* p. 323: "But back to the *point,* the chief point, the much-avoided point, the only point at issue: to abort is to destroy one's son or daughter."

More Pro-Life Materials from Liguori . . .

THE NINE-MONTH MIRACLE: A Journal for the Mother-to-Be
by Carrie J. Heiman

This book offers a joyful, prayerful meditation for each week of pregnancy and for the first few weeks following the child's birth. The meditations enhance the woman's experience of pregnancy and heighten her awareness of being a co-creator with God. Also included are blank pages for her personal thoughts — a place to record and save her own experience of the nine-month miracle. **$4.95**

DARE TO BE CHRISTIAN: Developing a Social Conscience
by Bernard Häring, C.SS.R.

For decades, world-renowned Father Bernard Häring has been teaching that God is love — and the only way to truly find God is to love people. In this book he helps Christians follow the example of Christ and reach out to others — to "be light to the world." His suggestions include: ● Share Your Faith ● Shape Public Opinion ● Give Youth a Chance ● Spread the Gospel of Peace. This book is a beautiful, simple invitation to see Christ by seeing the problems of others, to reach Christ by reaching out to others, to love Christ by loving others. **$4.25**

PRO-LIFE PAMPHLETS

ABORTION AND LAW: Questions People Ask

ARE NEWBORN BABIES BEING KILLED?: From Abortion to Infanticide

HOW ABORTION AFFECTS MEN: They Cry Alone

HOW ABORTION EXPLOITS WOMEN

THE SILENT SCREAMS: Abortion and Fetal Pain

(Each pamphlet is 24 pages in length, fits easily into a pocket or purse, and costs 50¢.

Order from your local bookstore or write to:
Liguori Publications, Box 060, Liguori, Missouri 63057-9999
(Please add 75¢ for postage and handling for first
item ordered and 25¢ for each additional item.)*
*For single pamphlet orders, send 50¢ plus a self-addressed, stamped envelope.